Education in a Competitive and Globalizing World

Exploring the Opportunities and Challenges of International Students

EDUCATION IN A COMPETITIVE AND GLOBALIZING WORLD

Additional books and e-books in this series can be found on Nova's website under the Series tab.

EDUCATION IN A COMPETITIVE AND GLOBALIZING WORLD

EXPLORING THE OPPORTUNITIES AND CHALLENGES OF INTERNATIONAL STUDENTS

MICHAEL ALLISON
EDITOR

Copyright © 2019 by Nova Science Publishers, Inc.

All rights reserved. No part of this book may be reproduced, stored in a retrieval system or transmitted in any form or by any means: electronic, electrostatic, magnetic, tape, mechanical photocopying, recording or otherwise without the written permission of the Publisher.

We have partnered with Copyright Clearance Center to make it easy for you to obtain permissions to reuse content from this publication. Simply navigate to this publication's page on Nova's website and locate the "Get Permission" button below the title description. This button is linked directly to the title's permission page on copyright.com. Alternatively, you can visit copyright.com and search by title, ISBN, or ISSN.

For further questions about using the service on copyright.com, please contact:
Copyright Clearance Center
Phone: +1-(978) 750-8400   Fax: +1-(978) 750-4470   E-mail: info@copyright.com.

NOTICE TO THE READER

The Publisher has taken reasonable care in the preparation of this book, but makes no expressed or implied warranty of any kind and assumes no responsibility for any errors or omissions. No liability is assumed for incidental or consequential damages in connection with or arising out of information contained in this book. The Publisher shall not be liable for any special, consequential, or exemplary damages resulting, in whole or in part, from the readers' use of, or reliance upon, this material. Any parts of this book based on government reports are so indicated and copyright is claimed for those parts to the extent applicable to compilations of such works.

Independent verification should be sought for any data, advice or recommendations contained in this book. In addition, no responsibility is assumed by the Publisher for any injury and/or damage to persons or property arising from any methods, products, instructions, ideas or otherwise contained in this publication.

This publication is designed to provide accurate and authoritative information with regard to the subject matter covered herein. It is sold with the clear understanding that the Publisher is not engaged in rendering legal or any other professional services. If legal or any other expert assistance is required, the services of a competent person should be sought. FROM A DECLARATION OF PARTICIPANTS JOINTLY ADOPTED BY A COMMITTEE OF THE AMERICAN BAR ASSOCIATION AND A COMMITTEE OF PUBLISHERS.

Additional color graphics may be available in the e-book version of this book.

Library of Congress Cataloging-in-Publication Data

ISBN: 978-1-53616-241-7

Published by Nova Science Publishers, Inc. † New York

CONTENTS

Preface		vii
Chapter 1	Through the Lens of Indigenous Psychology to a Taiwanese International Bicultural Model *Lei Wang, Shao-Jung 'Stella' Ko and Brian TaeHyuk Keum*	1
Chapter 2	Integrated Perspectives on Academic, Social and Psychological Adjustment among International Students *Sarifah Nurhanum Syed Sahuri and Rachel Wilson*	47
Chapter 3	Emotional Supports and Academic Stresses among Young Chinese International Students *Xi Lin, Shu Su and Alyssa McElwain*	77
Chapter 4	Great Expectations of Studying Abroad: Exchange Students from Umeå University, Sweden *Per A. Nilsson, Kerstin Westin and Dieter K. Müller*	99

Chapter 5	Exploring Challenges Faced by International Students in Computer Science Programs: Towards Understanding the Student Perspective *Michael J. Oudshoorn, Alison Clear, Janet Carter, Leo Hitchcock, Janice L. Pearce and Joseph A. Abandoh-Sam*	125
Index		**183**
Related Nova Publications		**187**

PREFACE

Exploring the Opportunities and Challenges of International Students opens with a focus on Taiwanese international students by defining the Taiwanese within historical and political context, providing an overview of the trends in studying abroad, as well as a literature review on Taiwanese international students' adjustment process.

Following this, the authors present an argument for integrating psychological, social and academic perspectives, highlighting the interrelation between these domains in empirical data collected using a new, integrated measure of students' academic, social and psychological adjustment.

Using a multi-university sample, the subsequent chapter presents a study of how types of emotional support play a role in how young Chinese international students' experience academic stresses.

In the penultimate study, in order to investigate students' expectations and experiences when studying abroad, a group of outbound exchange students at Umeå University, Sweden, were surveyed before and after the experience of studying in a foreign country.

In the concluding chapter, the authors examine the challenges faced by international students in integrating into computer science programs at various institutions, identifying differences in student and faculty perceptions.

Chapter 1 - International students are a growing population in the United States (U.S.). Students from Asia comprise approximately 69.2% of the total number of international students. Under this broad category of Asia, there are important within-group differences among Asian international students given the sociopolitical, geographic, and economic differences across diverse Asian countries that must be addressed in understanding their experiences in the U.S. This chapter specifically focuses on Taiwanese international students by providing a definition of Taiwanese within historical and political context, an overview of the trends in studying abroad, and a literature review on Taiwanese international students' adjustment process. In addition, the authors propose a Taiwanese International Bicultural Model (TIBM) derived from a review of indigenous psychology literature that incorporates underlying cultural factors. Three dimensions were identified in the TIBM: Priority Difference, Locus of Control, and Support Systems. Finally, implications for practice and future research are discussed to conclude this chapter.

Chapter 2 - The wellbeing of international students is central to the social good and economic productivity of international education across higher education institutions. As international students are the largest shareholder in the international education industry, their perspectives and interests need to be understood and protected. In particular, the challenges of adjusting to new circumstances in their host countries need to be understood so that programs can more fully support students. Substantial research maps out these challenges. However, research has tended to focus on psychological, social and academic adjustment as separate domains. The authors present an argument for integrating these perspectives; and they highlight the interrelation between these domains in empirical data collected using a new, integrated measure of students' academic, social and psychological adjustment among one international student population sample. The authors argue that sensitive exploration and surveying of these three inter-related domains of adjustment among specific sub-groups of international students, enables deeper understanding and empathy to be translated into supportive institutional practice that can be directly customised to those students' specific needs. Such an approach can contribute to more culturally sensitive, but holistically focussed, understanding of students, enabling them to flourish.

Chapter 3 - Using a multi-university sample, this chapter presents a study of how types of emotional support play a role in young Chinese international students' experience of academic stresses. A total number of 125 young Chinese sojourners who are aged between 18 to 26 participated in the study. Results indicate that a higher level of English proficiency, more parent involvement, and a lower level of loneliness reduce their academic stresses, while a closer friendship would increase their academic stresses. It is expected that this chapter will help higher education professionals to better understand and support today's young Chinese international students who study in the US. This chapter can further shed light on suggestions for higher education professionals both in the US and other countries to consider strategies to help young international students in their institutions.

Chapter 4 - The aim of this study is to investigate students' expectations and experiences when studying abroad. A group of outbound exchange students at Umeå University, Sweden, were surveyed before and after the experience of studying in a foreign country. The study is based on a panel of 57 students, who answered one questionnaire prior to leaving for studies abroad and another after six months when most had returned to Sweden. Overall, the students were satisfied with their stay abroad. While the findings are partly in line with previous studies – the students expected to develop their language skills, learn more about another culture, develop as a person, and use the experience as a merit in their future career – this study also showed that in some aspects their perception of studying abroad changed. Perceptions that changed between the questionnaires concerned courses not being offered at Umeå University, more courses being available abroad than at home, and change of environment; the students appreciated this change more than they had expected. Moreover, the willingness to work abroad after finishing the studies was assessed lower upon the return home after the time abroad. Swedish outbound exchange students can be characterized as participants in horizontal mobility, as they expect a foreign higher education institution (HEI) to be of similar quality as their home university, thus emphasizing personal development more than academic achievement.

Chapter 5 - International students are an important and desirable constituent in most computer science programs, bringing new perspectives into the classroom, diversifying the student population, globalizing the curriculum, broadening the perspective of domestic students, and often generating revenue for the host institution. Each of these characteristics is desirable and increasingly important in today's highly connected world and job market. Most institutions invest resources in attracting international students and providing support and orientation sessions for them on arrival to help acclimate them to the new environment and to introduce them to other students. Student clubs often provide support groups and social functions to help them meet and make friends with domestic students. However, challenges for international students, and for the faculty teaching them, persist at many institutions despite these efforts to help international students deal with culture shock, differing academic expectations and teaching methods, and different attitudes toward issues such as academic honesty. In this chapter, the authors examine the challenges faced by international students in integrating into computer science programs at various institutions, and explores these challenges and identifies differences in student and faculty perceptions. A survey of over 200 international students studying in four counties was conducted to gain insight into student perceptions of their educational experience.

In: Exploring the Opportunities …
Editor: Michael Allison

ISBN: 978-1-53616-241-7
© 2019 Nova Science Publishers, Inc.

Chapter 1

THROUGH THE LENS OF INDIGENOUS PSYCHOLOGY TO A TAIWANESE INTERNATIONAL BICULTURAL MODEL

Lei Wang[1],*, Shao-Jung 'Stella' Ko[2] and Brian TaeHyuk Keum[3]

[1]Graduate Psychology Program,
Chatham University, Pittsburgh, PA, US
[2]Department of Counseling Psychology, University of Denver,
Denver, CO, US
[3]Department of Counseling, Higher Education, and Special Education,
University of Maryland, College Park, MD, US

ABSTRACT

International students are a growing population in the United States (U.S.). Students from Asia comprise approximately 69.2% of the total number of international students. Under this broad category of Asia, there are important within-group differences among Asian international students

---

* Corresponding Author's Email: l.wang@chatham.edu.

given the sociopolitical, geographic, and economic differences across diverse Asian countries that must be addressed in understanding their experiences in the U.S. This chapter specifically focuses on Taiwanese international students by providing a definition of Taiwanese within historical and political context, an overview of the trends in studying abroad, and a literature review on Taiwanese international students' adjustment process. In addition, we propose a Taiwanese International Bicultural Model (TIBM; Figure 1) derived from a review of indigenous psychology literature that incorporates underlying cultural factors. Three dimensions were identified in the TIBM: Priority Difference, Locus of Control, and Support Systems. Finally, implications for practice and future research are discussed to conclude this chapter.

Keywords: Taiwanese international students, bicultural model, indigenous psychology

INTRODUCTION

International students are a growing population in the United States (U.S.; Institute of International Education, 2017a). The steady influx of international students has had a positive impact on the U.S. economy and educational system. In 2017-2018 international students contributed $39 billion to the economy of the U.S. (NAFSA: Association of International Educators, 2018). Additionally, international students bring cultural diversity into the classrooms. Cultural diversity in the classroom has been found to have a wide range of benefits, including students' learning outcomes, graduation rates, willingness to serve in underprivileged communities, personal income, post-college attainment (Gurin, Dey, Hurtado, & Gurin, 2002), openness to diversity, cognitive development, and self-confidence (Chang, Denson, Sáenz, & Misa, 2005). Chang and colleagues also noted that simply being immersed in a culturally diverse environment contributes to students' self-reported openness to diversity and cognitive development.

Asian international students comprise approximately 69.2% of the total number of international students studying in the U.S. (Institute of International Education, 2018). Some of the major countries of origin include China, India, South Korea, Taiwan, Vietnam, and Japan. Studies have shown that these students experience more cross-cultural barriers than their European counterparts, including higher levels of anxiety, lower self-efficacy in English, more perceived discrimination, and less social support (Chataway & Berry, 1989). Schmitt, Spears, and Branscombe (2003) suggested the importance of examining within-group differences among Asian international students given the sociopolitical, geographic, and economic differences across diverse Asian countries that must be addressed in understanding their unique experiences in the U.S.

Out of the top 10 countries of origin for all international students studying in the U.S., Taiwan is the smallest country in size. However, its students are overrepresented among international students on U.S. campuses, contributing approximately $774 million to the US economy (Institute of International Education, 2017b). A breakdown of the academic level showed that the majority of Taiwanese international students were pursuing a graduate degree (51%) and undergraduate degree (39%), while the rest of the individuals were non-degree seekers (Institute of International Education, 2018). While some scholars view Taiwanese as "ethnically Chinese" by aggregating Taiwanese and Chinese international students as one single population (e.g., Wang & Mallinckrodt, 2006; Wei et al., 2007), other researchers argue that Taiwanese international students are a distinct group (Swagler & Ellis, 2003). Given the distinct history of Taiwan (e.g., colonization and immigration), political environment, and the increasing trend of self-identification as "Taiwanese" rather than "Chinese" (Huang, 2016), we focus on examining the experiences of Taiwanese international students studying in the U.S. as an ethnic group in their own. A closer examination of this particular group is important for drawing implications for culturally-relevant services.

Studies have found that although international students experience many difficulties while studying in the U.S., they tend to view counseling as an inappropriate source for help (Nilsson, Berkel, Flores, & Lucas, 2004). Additionally, although Asian international students reported significantly higher levels of distress than North American and European international students who were studying in the U.S., Asian international students attended fewer counseling sessions than their European counterparts (Mitchell, Greenwood, & Guglielmi, 2007). Furthermore, those who seek out counseling often have a higher dropout rate after the initial session compared to U.S. students (Nilsson, Berkel, Flores, & Lucas, 2004). Scholars suggested that the lack of counselors' cultural sensitivity may dissuade students from continuing counseling (e.g., Zhang & Dixon, 2001). Meanwhile, many university counseling centers also struggle to find effective approaches to encourage international students to access services and to participate in counseling (Dipeolu, Kang, & Cooper, 2007). This highlights the importance of understanding the unique cross-national experiences of Taiwanese international students since the turn of the century, not only to provide culturally-relevant services to this population from the administration and counseling perspective, but also to derive implications for instructors and students who come into contact with these students both inside and outside the classroom.

In the following sections, this chapter provides the definition of Taiwanese and Taiwanese students' trend to study abroad to help the readers understand the background and context of this specific population. This chapter also provides a review of the literature on the adjustment issues that Taiwanese international students face when studying in the U.S. Because scholars (e.g., Swagler & Ellis, 2003) provided reviews of research on Taiwanese international students before the 2000s, this chapter examines peer-reviewed journal articles, master's theses, and doctoral dissertations on this population after the early 2000s. Comparison studies between Taiwanese and international students from other countries were also included. This chapter highlights the common outcomes (e.g., depression, stress, culture shock, acculturative stress, language anxiety) that scholars have utilized to quantitatively measure adjustment and the factors that are related to these outcomes. Further, this chapter also reviews the findings of qualitative research on this specific population. Finally, a Taiwanese International Bicultural Model derived from a review of indigenous psychology (i.e., cultural constructs that are unique to this population) is proposed to explain the underlying mechanisms that may be related to

Taiwanese international students' cross-national adjustment. Implications for research and practice are provided to conclude this chapter.

DEFINING TAIWANESE

Taiwan, also known as the Republic of China (ROC), is a nation located east of China on the Pacific Ocean. It is 13,974 square miles, with a population of 23.588932 in 2018 (Department of Statistics, 2018). Although 1949 was marked as the first official year that the Republic was established on the island, Taiwan has had a long-standing record of colonization and immigration since the 17th century.

The current Taiwanese population is considered multi-ethnic, with Han Chinese as the predominant group (95%; among them, approximately 70% Hokkien, 14% Hakka, and 14% Waishengren), while 2.3% are aboriginal Taiwanese (Central Intelligence Agency, 2019). Before the 17th century, aboriginal tribes inhabited the island. The Dutch and Spanish colonized the Southern and Northern parts of Taiwan, respectively, to conduct trade in the Eastern Hemisphere in the early 17th century. The island was later ruled by the Qing Dynasty of Mainland China from 1683 to 1895, the Japanese Empire from 1895 to 1945, and finally, the Nationalists from 1949 until the present day. Han Chinese immigrated to Taiwan primarily during the Qing Dynasty and after the Chinese Civil War in the late 1940s and early 1950s. More recently, there has been an influx of immigrants from China and Southeast Asia due to increased foreign spouses and workers.

It is also important to acknowledge that there has been a major shift in terms of how Taiwanese identify themselves. After the Chinese Civil War, the defeated Nationalists Party retreated to Taiwan and self-proclaimed as the "Republic of China" while the Communist Party as the "People's Republic of China." Both sides argued themselves as "China" (BBC, 2017). Because of this, older generations of Taiwanese individuals typically regarded themselves as "true" Chinese. Since President Lee acknowledged that the People's Republic of China is a separate entity from the Republic of China (Taiwan) in 1999 (Formosan Association for Public Affairs, 1999) and President Chen's support of Taiwan's independence in 2007 (林楠森, 2007 [Lin, 2007]), the Taiwanese identity became more prominent among younger generations as these political views were reflected in general educational materials starting from elementary school.

According to a recent survey conducted by National Chengchi University, 61% of respondents self-identified as Taiwanese (compared to 17.6% in 1992) and 24% supported the independence of Taiwan from China (Chen, 2017). The same survey showed 33% of participants identifying as both Taiwanese and Chinese (compared to 48% in 2004) and 4% considering themselves as solely Chinese (compared to 26% in 1994; Chen, 2017). In a survey of 1,084 participants who were phone-interviewed by Common Wealth Magazine, 62% considered themselves as Taiwanese only, 28% as both Taiwanese and Chinese, and 7% as Chinese only (林倖妃, 2017 [Lin, 2017]). The results also showed generational differences between age groups on how individuals identified themselves. A breakdown revealed that among 20 to 29-year old participants, 77% self-identified as Taiwanese only, whereas it was 67% among 30 to 39-year olds (林倖妃, 2017 [Lin, 2017]). Those who were younger than the age of 39 showed a preference for either "independence but keep peace with China" or "no matter what China does, Taiwan should be independent as soon as possible" (50% among 20 to 29-year old respondents and 54% among 30 to 39-year olds, respectively), which has exceeded the percentage of "maintain status quo (i.e., murky middle, no independence nor being a part of China)" for the first time (林倖妃, 2017 [Lin, 2017]). Even more recently, 1,074 participants were phone-interviewed by Focus Survey Research, indicating that only 25% of the Taiwanese public support the idea of "one country two systems," and 68% do not agree with China's "one-China principle" (Morgan, 2019). In addition, the results showed that 48% expect some kind of Taiwanese independence to take place in the future and only 22.7% expect unification (Morgan, 2019). Notably, there was a 12% increase of support towards Taiwan's independence between December 2018 and January 2019 after Chinese leader Xi Jinping made threats to the island. The same survey showed that 68% of respondents do not agree that China and Taiwan belong to "the same China" (Morgan, 2019). Although the issue between Taiwanese/Chinese identity and national identity is interrelated, in a latent class analysis, Huang (2005) confirmed that Taiwanese/Chinese identity and national identity are two analytically different dimensions, with four clusters: dual identifier, soft Taiwanese identifier, Chinese identifier, and hard Taiwanese identifier. Huang also reminded future researchers the potential danger of using the ethnicity of the fathers of participants as a default for ethnic identification as identity politics in Taiwan is considered multidimensional in nature.

Moreover, there has been a call for a separate checkbox for "Taiwanese" as an ethnicity option in the 2020 U.S. national census (Huang, 2016). This seems to suggest the strong connection and sense of belongingness that Taiwanese and Taiwanese Americans have towards their ethnic roots, which further highlights the importance of examining this group as a distinct ethnic group. We postulate that the negotiation between a Taiwanese and Chinese identity may be even more prominent for Taiwanese international students, especially when their nationality, race, and ethnicity are pronounced in a cross-national context, such as the U.S. We further hypothesize that these students may be more likely to perceive and interpret mislabeling them as "Chinese" to be discriminatory and/or oppressive, especially if they adhere strongly to a Taiwanese identity.

From a geographical, historical, and political standpoint, Taiwan and its inhabitants have been exposed to different cultures and mixed heritage ("Multicultural Taiwan"; Edmonson, 2009) which creates a unique worldview for this population. This distinctive worldview may also impact adjustment when Taiwanese international students are placed in a different context, such as the U.S. According to 陸洛 [Lu] (2011), in order to catch up with globalization (also seen as Westernization or post-colonialism), Taiwanese have adopted a "bicultural self." This bicultural self is the adaptation of individualism into collectivistic values; according to 陸洛 [Lu] (2011), this process is a reflection of integrating the self with new cultural values. 陸洛 [Lu] (2011) postulated that the development of a bicultural identity is a conscious process, meaning that the individuals are aware of what values and traits they choose to adopt in order to adapt to their environment. With this bicultural identity, Taiwanese international students may have better flexibility and more ways to cope with adjustment difficulties when studying in the US.

TREND IN STUDYING ABROAD IN THE U.S.

Studying abroad in the U.S. has become a trend in Taiwan since 1950 due to the encouragement of the government and economic growth. Funded by government scholarships, Taiwanese students were encouraged to pursue higher education in the U.S. in order to accelerate the development of the economy and technology in Taiwan (賴澤涵, 2013). Taiwanese international students' enrollment grew rapidly from 3,637 to 29,234 between 1949 to 2000, in which Taiwan remained the fifth most international students studying in the U.S. for half a century (Institute of International Education, 2010). However, the number gradually declined and maintained approximately 26,000 to 29,000 between 2000 and 2010 (Institute of International Education, 2010). The number of Taiwanese students then dropped significantly from 26,685 to 21,127 over a 5-year period (Institute of International Education, 2016), which possibly contributed to a significant loss in economic gains and classroom diversity in the U.S. (Institute of International Education, 2017b).

To better understand this trend, 賴澤涵 [Lai] (2013) and 戴肇洋 [Dai] (2005) found that the decline of Taiwanese students studying in the U.S. seems to be highly related to multiple reasons including (a) the change of the Taiwanese industrial structure and career trend (e.g., increased local entry-level employment opportunities in technology industry for college graduates), (b) better economy (e.g., better economic resources leading to higher quality of education in Taiwan), (c) spontaneity of the employers (e.g., numerous companies began to offer internship and practicum opportunities for undergraduate students, which has led to full-time employment at these placements upon graduation), (d) the positive potentials in China (e.g., less arduous application process, similar language and cultural contexts, and less expense in general), (e) funding issues (e.g., the increase in U.S. tuition and other fees, the strict requirements of Taiwanese government scholarships, and the competitive nature for funding between Taiwanese students and other foreign applicants for graduate assistantships), and (f) other personal concerns (e.g., English language proficiency, cultural adaptation, unpredictable acceptance rate of international students at U.S. institutes, unstable career trend in the home country, administrative bureaucracy of study abroad applications). In addition, most Taiwanese college graduates would rather stay in their home country, either attending local graduate schools or directly entering the workforce, as they perceived studying abroad to be full of barriers and costly (戴肇洋, 2005 [Dai, 2005]).

Furthermore, diplomatic and economic policies appear to affect Taiwanese students' willingness to study in the U.S. (梁明義、王文音, 2002 [Liang & Wang, 2002]). With the significant improvements in the economy, the Taiwanese government increased capacity to build better educational systems and resources across the country to promote greater accessibility of higher education (戴肇洋, 2005 [Dai, 2005]). These efforts encouraged Taiwanese young adults to develop and carry out their career plans without having to afford the high expenses of studying abroad (戴肇洋, 2005 [Dai, 2005]). In addition, the decline in the number of Taiwanese international students studying in the U.S. may also be partially explained by the Taiwanese government's encouragement to study in other Asian countries. Since the late 20th century, the Taiwanese government began to support students' pursuit in higher education in the U.S. with the condition that individuals return to Taiwan to engage in government affairs or take on teaching and research duties at Taiwanese universities. From 2000 to 2016, three presidents, including President Chen (2000-2008), President Ma (2008-2016), and President Tsai (2016-present), have taken different political and economic approaches that may have impacted the policies and funding to study abroad. President Chen supported more post-doctoral fellows and short-term researchers to pursue higher education in the U.S., with the hopes of accelerating the development of technology (鄭如雲, 2007

[Cheng, 2007]). Unlike President Chen, President Ma started to strengthen educational cooperation with China, South or Southeast Asian countries by recognizing each other's college degrees and establishing exchange or dual-degree programs. To accomplish this, the government reduced the amount of scholarship available for studying in the U.S. Recently, President Tsai continued this policy and developed a "New South Direction Plan" to encourage Taiwanese students to study in the ten countries that are members of the Association of Southeast Asian Nations. Overall, the decreased funding and reduced opportunities for government sponsorship may have affected Taiwanese students' willingness to study in the U.S. (戴肇洋, 2005 [Dai, 2005]), which in turn may have contributed to the decline of Taiwanese international students in the U.S.

In addition to funding issues, cultural factors may also play an influential role in Taiwanese students' career decision-making process. Although the within-group differences among Asian countries exist, Taiwan and other Asian countries still share more similarities (e.g., cultural values, emphasis on collectivism) than between Taiwan and the U.S. It is understandable that some Taiwanese students would choose to study abroad in other Asian countries rather than the U.S. perhaps due to consideration of less effort in adapting to a new cultural environment (戴肇洋, 2005 [Dai, 2005]). Considering that adjustment requires time and effort, such as the development of coping strategies, it is essential to explore and better understand the cross-national experience among Taiwanese international students from various aspects (e.g., academic, social, daily functioning, negative and positive psychological outcomes).

ADJUSTMENT AMONG TAIWANESE INTERNATIONAL STUDENTS IN THE US

Much of the quantitative research has focused on negative psychological outcomes as a way to assess the adjustment of Taiwanese international students. However, this pathological view may discount the positive psychological outcomes and limit assessing adjustment from a more holistic point of view (Keyes, 2005). Keyes highlighted the importance of separating positive and negative psychological outcomes by postulating the complete state model of mental health and mental illness. In other words, the two concepts should be examined separately and not to be assumed that the absence of one means the existence of the other (Keyes, 2005). Therefore, we draw upon this model to gain a more complete picture of Taiwanese international students' psychological outcomes; thus, we structure this section into two main parts—mental illness and mental health. Moreover, we have included a section that summarizes findings from qualitative research as there seems to be a trend of examining Taiwanese international students' experience using qualitative approaches.

Mental Illness

In this chapter, mental illness includes what can be considered as negative psychological symptoms, such as depression, stress, culture shock, acculturative stressors, and language anxiety that Taiwanese international students experience as they cross borders to study in the U.S.

Depression

Several studies examined factors that are associated with depressive symptoms. Dao, Lee, and Chang (2007) found that among Taiwanese international graduate students, those at risk for depressive feelings were more likely to be female, less acculturated, and those who have lower perceived English fluency. Dao and colleagues also found that perceived English fluency fully mediated the relationship between acculturation level and depression for both males and females, with perceived English fluency having a negative and significant association with depression. Among graduate students, Ying and Han (2006) found in their longitudinal study that extroversion diminished depressive symptoms, while acculturative stressors reduced functional adjustment and increased endorsement of depressive symptoms. Collectively, the studies suggest that Taiwanese international students may be more at risk for depressive symptoms if they perceive themselves as less acculturated to the U.S. and struggling with English.

Stress

Yang (2010) examined the relationship between graduate school stress (i.e., academic stress, environmental stress, and family/monetary stress), coping, and mental health among a sample of graduate students from the U.S., Taiwan, China, and Korea. The results showed that international students from Taiwan and Korea generally had higher graduate school stress compared to domestic U.S. students. Yang (2010) found that culture was significantly correlated with maladaptive coping, especially among Taiwanese international students. Results indicated that the Asian international students were not homogenous regarding stress levels, psychological outcomes, and ways of coping. More specifically, Taiwanese international students tend to adopt coping strategies (i.e., self-distraction, denial, venting, substance use, behavioral disengagement, and self-blame) that would be considered maladaptive in the U.S. context and yet reported good mental health (Yang, 2010).

Culture Shock and Acculturative Stressors

Culture shock adaptation was found to be predicted by communication apprehension about English and social contact balance with both domestic and other Taiwanese international students, but not by TOEFL scores (Swagler & Ellis, 2003). Among Taiwanese international graduate students in a longitudinal study, Ying (2005) found that the length of stay in the U.S. predicted the intensity of acculturative stressors. Specifically, acculturative stressors (i.e., homesickness, cultural difference, social isolation, academics, and unfamiliar climate) were more intense early on but dissipated over time (Ying, 2005). Stressors related to academic challenges and unfamiliarity with the climate were significantly reduced from the fall to spring semesters of the first academic year, whereas stressors pertaining to homesickness, cultural difference, and social isolation were decreased from the spring semester of the first academic year to the fall semester in the following year

(Ying, 2005). Ying explained that academics is the sole reason for Taiwanese international students to travel to the U.S.; therefore, it would be the first concern they would try to cope with and other stressors may be of less priority. The author also mentioned that some Taiwanese students may prepare and anticipate their adjustment to the U.S. culture prior to coming over which may explain why they may have been less susceptible to "culture shock." In addition, Ying highlighted that the timing of outreach and programming efforts should target pre-arrival and orientation.

Language Anxiety

Language anxiety is considered a type of social anxiety that is dependent upon the learner's interactions with others (Pappamihiel, 2002). Huang (2009) found that among Taiwanese graduate students, listening comprehension (including speech rate), participation in group discussion, and grammatical errors in writing are primarily related to language anxiety and adjustment in U.S. classrooms. Perceived attitudes of domestic students, listening and speaking related skills, and loneliness/isolation are related to language anxiety and adjustment outside of the classroom (Huang, 2009). To actively cope with these learning-related issues, participants sought help from classmates and professors, visited the writing center, and paid for editorial services (Huang, 2009). The participants also made an effort to speak more and watch local television shows to overcome the fear of losing face due to English language fluency (Huang, 2009).

A review of the literature on mental illness and adjustment among Taiwanese international students indicate that scholars examined different aspects of participants' experiences. One key aspect that seems to be missing from the literature is the negotiation of the Taiwanese and Chinese identity and how this is related to psychological outcomes. We next review the literature on mental health and adjustment among this population.

Mental Health

Scholars have criticized the emphasis placed on the deficit model of pathology and maladjustment when examining the experiences of international students (Bochner, Furnham, & Ward, 2001). There is a trend to take a developmental perspective as well as attention on environmental factors that may come into play (e.g., Earley & Ang, 2003; Hammer, Bennett, & Wisemer, 2003; Heppner, Wang, Heppner, & Wang, 2012). Therefore, in this section we review literature on positive psychological outcomes related to the adjustment of Taiwanese international students.

Satisfaction with Life

In a sample of 121 undergraduate and graduate Taiwanese international students, Wang, Wang, Heppner, and Chuang (2016) found that cross-national cultural competence (i.e., "an individual's capability to function and manage effectively in culturally diverse settings"; Ang et al., 2007, p. 336) significantly and positively mediated the relationship between several predictors (i.e., personality, immersion experience, and cultural reflection factors) and satisfaction with life, but not between predictors and psychological distress. Satisfaction with life was measured by the Satisfaction with Life Scale (Diener, Emmons, Larsen, & Griffen, 1985). This finding is congruent with the complete state model of health that Keyes (2005) postulated in that mental health and mental illness do not exist on a unidimensional spectrum.

Functional Adjustment

A few longitudinal studies examined functional adjustment (i.e., participants' subjective view of how they are adjusting to life in the U.S.). Ying and Han (2006) found that social affiliation with domestic U.S. students during the second semester partially and positively mediated the effect of extroversion on functional adjustment. Functional adjustment was measured by three items: "*How well are you adjusting to living in the U.S.?*" "*How do you feel about living in the U.S.?*" and "*How do you feel about studying in the U.S.?*" The responses were coded on a 5-point Likert scale ranging from 1 (*not well at all*) to 5 (*very well*). In another longitudinal study, Ying and Han (2008) found that self-reported ethnic density (i.e., participants reported on a 4-point Likert scale from "*few*" to "*very many*" their subjective views of how many other Taiwanese international students there were on campus) predicted the adjustment of Taiwanese international graduate students. Specifically, the results showed that students on campuses with fewer Taiwanese international peers formed more relationships with domestic students and developed greater English fluency by the second semester compared to those who were on campuses with more Taiwanese peers. In addition, homesickness, affiliation with domestic students, and subjective English competence in the second semester predicted functional adjustment in the third semester among participants at schools with moderate ethnic density, while baseline subjective English fluency predicted adjustment in participants at high ethnic density schools. However, the presence of a Taiwanese ethnic community did not significantly reduce acculturative stressors for the students at high ethnic density campuses (Ying & Han, 2008).

Cross-National Cultural Competency

Wang and colleagues (2016) found that personality (i.e., perseverance, curiosity, and exploration), immersion experiences (i.e., social connectedness with mainstream and ethnic community, perceived language discrimination, length of stay, and subjective English proficiency), and cultural reflection factors, except TOEFL scores, were significantly related to cross-national cultural competency. Cross-national cultural competency was also found to be significantly associated with both satisfaction with life and depression, but not anxiety.

Acculturation

Shih and Brown (2000) explored the relationship between acculturation level and vocational identity among a group of graduate and undergraduate Taiwanese international students. The results revealed that those who were older and had shorter length of stay in the U.S. were more likely to score higher as Asian identified. In addition, lower acculturation level and being older were also related to having a higher vocational identity. However, the scale used in the study postulated that acculturation is unidimensional instead of multidimensional which is accepted as more appropriate to measure the adoption of mainstream and ethnic culture nowadays (Herskovits, 1948; LaFromboise, Coleman, & Gerton, 1993).

By utilizing the complete state model (Keyes, 2005), scholars are better able to identify and understand how different variables relate to both mental illness and mental health. One of the shortcomings of quantitative research is the lack of understanding of the process that Taiwanese international students experience when adapting to US culture. Therefore, it is essential to also review qualitative studies that address this issue.

Qualitative Approaches Examining the Adjustment Process

Results from qualitative studies are reviewed in this chapter, as there seems to be a trend toward using such approaches to better understand the in-depth lived experiences of Taiwanese international students. Qualitative researchers are expected to approach the field "without being constrained by predetermined categories of analysis, which will contribute to the depth, openness, and detail of qualitative inquiry" (Patton, 2002, p. 14). The studies reviewed below generally fall into three themes: general adaptation, identities and English names, and learning styles.

General Adaptation

Swagler and Ellis (2003) interviewed 25 Taiwanese international students pursuing graduate school at a mid-sized Northeastern university in the U.S. on issues pertaining to adjustment. The participants were 14 men and 10 women, who came from varying majors, ages, and six different cities of origin in Taiwan. The semi-structured interviews were conducted in English due to the authors' limited proficiency in Mandarin Chinese. The authors acknowledged that some of the participants at times struggled to express themselves. Common themes using a phenomenological method revealed that confidence in speaking English, social connections with

Taiwanese and domestic students, and the ability to be independent were related to their cross-national adjustment. In their focus group, participants reported having to cross the cultural distance between U.S. and Taiwanese cultures when establishing interpersonal connections, language barriers, and cultural differences between student-teacher relationships and the nature of individualism versus collectivism between the two cultures (Swagler & Ellis, 2003). Similarly, in a phenomenological study with eight Taiwanese exchange students who have returned to Taiwan, Lee, Bei, and DeVaney (2007) found that participants were aware of the lower power differences between students and teachers in the U.S. Participants also reported noticing the different ways that U.S. peers used to cope with uncertainty (e.g., being more relaxed and unafraid to ask questions) and individualistic behaviors (e.g., valuing personal lives). Participants were able to adjust to the classroom culture and performed well even though they were initially anxious. The interviews were conducted in Mandarin Chinese, transcribed into English, and participants were asked to conduct member check on the accuracy of translations.

A qualitative study using a case study approach conducted by Pham (2013) examined factors that were related to social and academic integration (i.e., involvement in social and academic activities, interpersonal relationships with other students and faculty) among 14 Taiwanese, Korean, and Malaysian full-time international undergraduate students in their third year. Data were collected across two interviews per participants with one to two weeks apart. Pham concluded that participants' limited cultural awareness, knowledge of the U.S. and its educational system, and language proficiency for engaging in cross-cultural interactions were key factors that affected social and academic integration. Most participants were more academically integrated than socially. Taiwanese and Malaysian students were more likely to be academically and socially integrated than Korean students.

Identities and English Names

Identity is considered a fluid concept as it is considered developmental, dynamic, continuous, and a complex process (Huang, 2014). Edmondson

(2009) examined how Taiwanese international students across different generations have negotiated the identity of being "Chinese" or "Taiwanese" and how the political climate in Taiwan has evolved and influenced their identification. Using narrative inquiry, Huang (2014) explored how 15 Taiwanese international doctoral students developed a sense of ethnic identity due to experiencing discrepancies between in-country identity (i.e., Taiwanese) and out-of-country identity (i.e., Chinese). The participants were seven men and eight women who stayed in the U.S. for more than two years at various universities across the U.S. They expressed discomfort and feeling offended by being mislabeled as "Chinese." The participants refused to be labeled as Chinese as they argued that Taiwanese and Chinese are inherently different. Huang (2014) also found that the individuals identified their ethnic identity in two primary ways: (1) by where they were born and raised, and (2) by their ancestral heritage (i.e., parents' ethnicity). While the former indicated that the participants equated their nationality with their ethnicity (i.e., Taiwanese), the latter showed that participants valued their ethnic roots as well as where they grew up (e.g., Filipino-Taiwanese and Vietnamese-Taiwanese).

Adoption of English names for Taiwanese international students appeared at first to be governed by personal choice and was found to be constrained by linguistic and social factors (Wu, 2014). Among ten Taiwanese international students at a large public university on the West Coast, Chen (2013) found that the practice begins in Taiwan and is continued when they come to the U.S., which helps them transform from outsiders to insiders (i.e., gaining acceptance in the host culture) as well as influence acculturation (Chen, 2013). In a qualitative study, Wu (2014) explored the adoption of English names among Taiwanese international students using a phenomenological approach. Participants (six men and six women) believed that not being concerned about maintaining ethnic names may be influenced by their national and ethnic identities. Interview questions were asked in English and any response in Mandarin Chinese were translated into English during transcription. Wu (2014) believed that adopting English names is a sign of both assimilation and acculturation (i.e., code-switching). Specifically, participants were still using their Chinese names in Taiwan and

English names in the U.S. Their English names served two purposes: (a) to reduce embarrassment for others who may not be able to pronounce their names, and (b) to increase contact with domestic students because their English names may be easier to remember. Wu (2014) further postulated that adopting English names does not necessarily mean that the participants abandoned their Taiwanese roots. This may indicate that the participants formed a bicultural identity that assisted them to navigate between the two different cultural contexts. Adopting an English name for Taiwanese international students served a different purpose than students from Hong Kong who used English names as part of their post-colonial identity and a way to differentiate themselves from mainland Chinese (e.g., Chan, 2002).

Learning Styles

Lin (2004) used a phenomenological method to explore the expectations of learning and teaching among eight Taiwanese social science graduate students attending a large public university on the East Coast, how these expectations differed from American teachers, and how these participants coped with the difference in expectations. The participants were two men and two women who had studied for less than a year at the university and two men and two women who had studied longer than a year. Interviews were conducted in Mandarin Chinese. Data analysis revealed that the students tend to be uncritical in learning (i.e., does not challenge instructors or criticize ideas) and passive in class participation, which was the opposite to what they perceived as U.S. teachers' expectations. Five themes were identified that caused the difference in expectations about learning and teaching: authority in power, learner autonomy, the power issue, the face issue, and group harmony. These differences had a negative impact on participants' cross-cultural adjustment. To cope with the differences, participants adjusted their learning strategy and modified their attitudes and values towards learning. For instance, by becoming more proactive in class, studying even harder to meet their U.S. teachers' expectations and handling heavy coursework, and taking a more critical approach (Lin, 2004).

In general, most of the qualitative studies that specifically focused on Taiwanese international students surveyed their participants in Mandarin

Chinese, whereas comparative research was conducted in English. However, only one study (Wang et al., 2016) specifically laid out how the measures were translated and back-translated using the method suggested by Brislin (1980). In addition, most of the qualitative studies took a phenomenological approach to better capture the experiences of Taiwanese international students regarding their adjustment in the U.S. Although the development of identities (e.g., ethnic, nationality, and cultural) were explored, there seems to be a lack of focus on culture-specific concepts that may contribute to their resilience. There is also a lack of literature examining the extent to which Taiwanese international students' experience discrimination or oppression when being mislabeled as "Chinese" by others. Therefore, a new model is proposed in this chapter to address this gap in the literature and better explain the adjustment process among Taiwanese students.

TAIWANESE INTERNATIONAL BICULTURAL MODEL: MOVING FROM PROBLEM TO RESILIENCE

Cultural distance (i.e., the extent of similarities and differences of cultures; Shenkar, 2001) between the U.S. and Asian countries is typically considered relatively large and has been identified to affect international students' adjustment to the U.S. culture (Redmond, 2000). Triandis (1995) postulated a commonly accepted definition of collectivism and highlighted that individuals in collectivistic societies (a) view themselves as part of one or more collectives (e.g., family, community), (b) are motivated by group norms, (c) are willing to prioritize the group over self, and (d) value connectedness to others. However, this broad conceptualization of collectivism may not take into consideration the complexities of the context of countries that have a history of colonization and immigration in addition to the influence of globalization.

LaFromboise and colleagues (1993) proposed a biculturalism model that places emphasis on bicultural competence. Biculturalism is significantly different from acculturation because it posits a bidirectional and orthogonal relationship between culture-of-origin and the second culture. The two cultures also do not necessarily have a hierarchical relationship. Therefore, the individual has the autonomy to choose which culture they identify and adhere to more. In order to be biculturally competent, LaFromboise and colleagues (1993) believe that the individual may need to possess (a) knowledge of cultural beliefs and values, (b) positive attitudes toward both groups, (c) bicultural efficacy, (d) communication ability, (e) role repertoire, and (f) a sense of groundedness. Taiwanese, for instance, have been theorized to possess a bicultural identity that includes both individualism and collectivism (陸洛, 2011 [Lu, 2011]). This bicultural identity is considered to be fluid, and it changes based upon upbringing and environment and may be conducive to being more flexible in regards to acculturation and coping in a new environment such as in the U.S. Moreover, it is likely that Taiwanese individuals from bigger cities are exposed to greater levels of individualistic values. Yet, Taiwanese society, in general, may place a greater value on high context (i.e., communication happens more through nonverbal communication; Sue & Sue, 2015), which creates an environment that holds onto traditional social and interpersonal expectations and continues to coexist with individualistic values. This coexistence was demonstrated through factor analyses of personality assessment. Scholars found that measurement of the Big Five personalities in a mixed sample of Taiwanese and Chinese individuals yielded seven dimensions. The Big Seven Personalities included competence vs. impotence, industriousness vs. unindustriousness, other-oriented vs. self-centeredness, agreeableness vs. disagreeableness, extraversion vs. introversion, large-mindedness vs. small-mindedness, and contentedness vs. vaingloriousness. All personalities were related to interpersonal patterns, which was vastly different from the individual-focused personalities among Western participants (楊國樞, 1999 [Yang, 1991]). In addition, Hsu, Wang, and Yang (2001) found that participants from Taiwan scored higher on contentedness than their Chinese counterparts. Collectively, the author highlighted the importance of examining cross-cultural differences (e.g., socioeconomic and cultural traditions) between the two groups.

While the literature on Taiwanese international students tends to focus on a variety of adjustment issues, there is a gap between these issues and the underlying mechanisms that help students cope. In other words, there is a lack of application of cultural concepts or factors specific to Taiwanese international students. Therefore, it is essential to examine the literature of indigenous psychology to better understand what psychological variables may be at play, especially those pertaining to resilience when considering adjustment of Taiwanese international students in the U.S. Based on the literature, we propose a Taiwanese International Bicultural Model (Figure 1) with three dimensions (priority difference, locus of control, and support systems) in an effort to better understand the mechanisms that come into play when considering the cross-national experiences and help-seeking considerations and behaviors of individuals from Taiwan. The dimensions of the framework are further elaborated in the following sections.

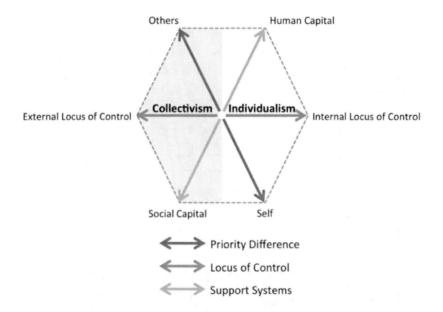

Figure 1. The three dimensions of the Taiwanese International Bicultural Model.

Priority Difference

The first dimension is the priority difference between Taiwanese and U.S. individuals when it comes to decision-making, which affects interpersonal relationships and how individuals prioritize their own or others' needs. People in individualistic society typically learn to make decisions for themselves and take responsibility for their own lives, whereas individuals with a collectivistic background pay more attention to the needs and requests of others.

Group Harmony
The core element of collectivism is the assumption that individuals are bound and committed to groups (Oyserman, Coon, & Kemmelmeier, 2002). As individuals from the same cultural values share similar priorities (self versus others), they create their own networks to easily socialize to new educational or occupational circumstances. One's career or academic development is significantly affected by the closeness with others, which determines the resources and assistance one can obtain (Bian, 2001; Heggins & Jackson, 2003). Thus, it is important to maintain harmonious interpersonal relationships with one another to guarantee one's own support system and future development.

Within a harmonious interpersonal relationship, Taiwanese are willing to support each other and empathize with different viewpoints (Lin, 2017). Oyserman and colleagues (2002) argue that a collectivistic individual conceptualizes the self as a part of a larger group and prioritizes interpersonal harmony over individual autonomy. To maintain harmonious interpersonal relationships and positive self-images (called "mien-tzu" or commonly known as "face" in Western literature), Taiwanese may strive to value "others" more than the "self" through cooperative interpersonal interactions. In a cross-cultural comparison study, Taiwanese undergraduate students reported lower levels of argumentativeness than their domestic peers to avoid uncomfortable feelings and maintain group harmony (Hsu, 2007). From this, we postulate that Taiwanese international students would try their best to respond to others' needs, whereas their domestic counterparts may consider themselves first, set boundaries, and express their needs in a clear manner. This difference becomes especially obvious when a conflict of interest occurs between individuals and groups, as most individuals from a collectivistic background tend to sacrifice personal convenience to show respect and avoid disharmony (Oyserman et al., 2002). For example, in a group project setting, it is possible that Taiwanese international students would rather take on more tasks themselves rather than directly reminding or confronting their domestic peers to be responsible for the unfinished group work.

Forbearance

Unlike their individualistic peers who may be more used to expressing their opinions and requests directly, Taiwanese international students with a collectivistic background are more likely to repress their personal needs with the purpose of maintaining group harmony (Hwang, 1977). To avoid the risk of ruining group harmony, they present a positive and cooperative image of themselves by prioritizing others' benefits first. For example, Taiwanese international students may not feel comfortable asking for help from others frequently, as they may worry about becoming a burden, fear of disturbing others, and being viewed in a negative light. Taiwanese international students also may feel uncomfortable in rejecting others, or even guilty when prioritizing personal benefits. In order to avoid being labeled or perceived as arrogant or uncooperative, Taiwanese international students may try to forbear and suppress their own needs.

Normally, either tendency of priority (self versus others) may work effectively when the individuals involved have an understanding of everyone's intentions in order to negotiate and strike a balance among everyone's needs. However, Taiwanese international students may encounter interpersonal difficulties at the beginning of their experience in the U.S. due to cross-cultural differences and expectations. For example, when scheduling a meeting time for group study, Taiwanese students may try their best to fit into others' schedules and adjust accordingly, whereas domestic students may voice their preferred time slots and possibly change the meeting time so that it fits better with their schedules. Given this discrepancy, Taiwanese students may feel disrespected, confused, or angry at their domestic peers' individualistic behaviors, whereas domestic students may feel confused about why Taiwanese international students do not speak up about their scheduling needs. Different priorities may potentially lead to different expectations that could affect how Taiwanese students adapt to the U.S. culture and whether they will successfully establish meaningful cross-cultural relationships with domestic students.

Locus of Control

Locus of control is the extent to which individuals believe they have control over their lives (Sue & Sue, 2015). Individuals with a higher internal locus of control have been found to possess more perfectionistic tendencies, whether adaptive or maladaptive, because they believe that they have control over the process and outcomes (Periasamy & Ashby, 2002). They may also be more problem-solving oriented and proactive when seeking help (Ross & Mirowsky, 1989), leading them to be more resourceful. From a Western perspective, it is typically believed that individuals who possess an external locus of control are maladaptive because they are more passive and do not assume responsibility for their choices and consequences (Periasamy & Ashby, 2002). A review of the indigenous psychology literature shows that there are several concepts that may be related to external locus of control, and in fact may be valued and considered adaptive in Taiwan (Tone, 2002). Such traits include forbearance, "go with the flow," and reframing.

Forbearance, mentioned in the previous section, may also come into play when considering locus of control. Individuals who adopt greater external locus of control tend to believe that their negative situation would soon change as long as they are able to endure such hardships (Sue & Sue, 2015). Taiwanese international students may try to let go of difficult situations by minimizing and rationalizing internally in order to save face so that they are not perceived as weak or whiny and maintain interpersonal harmony. Although forbearance share similarities with perseverance, it would be helpful for mental health prevention specialists and practitioners to teach students how to recognize the costs and not to delay help-seeking if needed. In addition, scholars have identified the importance of being more flexible when it comes to forbearance in order to be more adaptive (Lin, Huang, & Lee, 2011). For instance, being able to recognize the quality of the interpersonal relationship may help Taiwanese international students decide if the situation is safe for confrontation or if it would be best to keep to oneself and seek assistance elsewhere (Lin et al., 2011).

"Going with the flow" (seeking synchronization with the universe; Tone, 2002) is a common pursuit for Taiwanese individuals who affiliate themselves with indigenous religions, which is related to the strong belief in fate and life trajectories being controlled by higher powers. Examples of such pursuits may include seeking fortune tellers and practicing mindfulness meditations. In terms of going with the flow under interpersonal circumstances, a study found that Taiwanese individuals tend to exert less assertiveness when they sense power differences between themselves and others while they assert themselves more when they feel the power is more equal (Kao, 2013). However, the same study found that Taiwanese individuals tend to go with the flow more than being assertive (Kao, 2013). It is likely that possessing a higher external locus of control leads to reframing (e.g., believing that hardships or unsuccessful attempts are due to fate), which then leads to self-compassion and resilience in cross-cultural scenarios.

Support Systems

Previous research found systematic differences in the frequency of support seeking between people from individualistic and collectivistic cultures (Hwang, 2006; Mizuno & Ishikuma, 1999; Mojaverian, Hashimoto, & Kim, 2012). The support system is typically divided into two aspects: social capital and human capital. Social capital refers to the resource embedded in people's social networks that can provide purposeful functions to increase success in both academic and vocational fields (Hwang, 1977; Yan & Lam, 2009). Human capital refers to an asset generated by investment in education, training, and medical care (Becker, 1964). Human capital support includes professional experts outside of support seekers' immediate personal social networks who have been trained or possess useful resources to deal with particular concerns, such as medical doctors and psychologists.

Studies have shown that individuals from collectivistic cultures are generally unlikely to seek support from counselors, mental health practitioners, institutions, or professionals (Cortina, 2004; Shek, 1998). Instead, collectivistic members tend to seek support from their spouses, family members, close friends, and other in-group members with whom they have formed a close bond (Feng, 2015). In particular, Shin (2002) found that Taiwanese individuals are less likely to seek professional assistance than those in individualistic cultures. Therefore, Taiwanese international students may be more likely to utilize their social capital than human capital. For instance, friends and family are part of one's social capital and may be willing to provide assistance due to closeness in their relationships; however, they may or may not possess the best problem-solving strategies or readily available professional resources. Unlike their Taiwanese counterparts who tend to view advice-seeking as a way to deepen and maintain their relationships with close friends and family, domestic students tend to use advice-seeking as a general social strategy to make connections with anyone, including professionals who may not necessarily be their close friends or family (Oyserman et al., 2002).(Shin, 2002). Thus, it is crucial to explore the reasons behind this phenomenon in order to make professional resources more accessible for Taiwanese international students and strike a balance between utilizing the two different support systems. We next discuss the elements that make up social capital for Taiwanese international students, namely ren-qing and mien-tzu.

Ren-qing

Ren-qing is an essential factor in interpersonal relationships that motivates people to fulfill their obligations towards others as part of the maintenance of group harmony (鄭伯壎, 1999). In fact, ren-qing is not a pattern that only exists in collectivism, but is also conceptualized as "indebtedness" in Western cultures (Greenberg, 1980) defined as a state of obligation to repay others. People learn the concepts of altruism and reciprocity from the process of socialization and feel uncomfortable when receiving help without returning the favor. Thus, indebtedness has motivational properties--the greater the reluctance and discomfort from receiving interpersonal help, the stronger the ensuing attempts to reduce it and return the favor in order to restore the balance of power in relationships (Greenberg, 1980).

Although members from both individualistic and collectivistic cultures are influenced by the concept of interpersonal obligations, ren-qing acts as a determining role in collectivistic cultures that affects the decision-making process for support-seeking. Studies show that in relationships with greater closeness or intimate rapport, people feel less indebted and discomfort when receiving a favor; conversely, feelings of indebtedness and obligatory guilt is stronger when people receive favors from strangers or acquaintances. The latter may explain why Taiwanese individuals are reluctant to seek help from unfamiliar professionals (林宜旻, 2004 [Lin, 2004]). Accordingly, it is possible that Taiwanese international students will experience discomfort and guilt when seeking help from institutions or resourceful authorities as they may feel that they are unable to reciprocate. Therefore, they may rather go to their close friends or family members whom they feel more comfortable to rely on.

Mien-tzu

Another factor that impacts collectivistic members' support-seeking decision is the concept of mien-tzu, which is commonly referred to as "face" in Western literature but actually is a different concept in Taiwanese indigenous psychology. According to Hu (1994), face is considered as the respect in morals or ethics while mien-tzu refers to the good reputation built by one's personal efforts. King and Myers (1977) also suggested replacing face and mien-tzu with "moral face" and "social face," respectively, as they have been misused for the same concept. According to 韓貴香、李美枝 [Han and Li] (2011), Taiwanese would rather turn to human capital (e.g., professionals) when they can foresee their mien-tzu being potentially jeopardized if they sought help from their social capital (e.g., friends and family). In other words, when Taiwanese international students feel a threat of losing social face from those with whom they are familiar, they will then consider seeking help from professionals to feel less ashamed or to maintain their reputation. This contradicts the assumption that Taiwanese international students will be less likely to seek professional help for psychological concerns than those from individualistic cultures.

Although ren-qing (indebtedness) and mien-tzu (reputation) exist in both Taiwanese and individualistic cultures, they hold different weight among the cultures and can affect the acculturation process to varying degrees. Taiwanese international students may seek help from family and friends, though less professional, rather than visiting professionals due to the pressures of ren-qing. Nevertheless, if there are concerns for their mien-tzu being jeopardized, they may then seek help from professional sources. We believe that this dilemma may be most directly related to how mental health practitioners can assist Taiwanese international students with their adjustment in the U.S. and psychological help-seeking.

Nationality, Race, and Ethnicity

Intersectionality of nationality, race, and ethnicity is a unique aspect in the Taiwanese International Bicultural Model. In a framework of racial identity development for international students, Fries-Britt, Mwangi, and Peralta (2014) postulated the importance of considering the racial/ethnic identities that were previously developed in the context of their home countries. While in Taiwan, Taiwanese international students may identify with a particular racial (e.g., Han) and ethnic group (e.g., Hakka). When they cross borders into the U.S., they encounter issues around nationality and race in addition to ethnicity. This may mean having to negotiate between identities and choosing which one(s) to identify with and/or represent. Depending on how individuals perceive their Taiwanese/Chinese and national identities (Huang, 2005), this identity adoption and adjustment may influence how Taiwanese international students choose to adhere to collectivistic or individualistic values. For instance, individuals who identify as "hard" Taiwanese, may choose to adhere to more individualistic values in order to demonstrate that they are different from Chinese international students from Mainland China. The negotiation and incorporation of nationality and ethnicity is considered "dual identity" and has been utilized in intergroup relations and acculturation studies (Fleischmann & Verkuyten, 2016).

IMPLICATIONS

Given the historical, geographical, and political context of Taiwan, it is important to consider Taiwanese international students studying in the U.S. as a distinct population rather than treating them under the broad "Chinese" umbrella. According to Yang and Lu (2005), Taiwanese individuals are likely to develop a bicultural identity under the influence of both Eastern and Western cultures present in Taiwan. This bicultural identity is also dependent upon upbringing and childhood experiences, as individuals may adopt varying levels of collectivistic or individualistic values (韓桂香, 2003 [Han, 2003]). A review of literature on Taiwanese international students in the U.S. reveals that studies tend to focus less on cultural factors when examining issues around adjustment and more on the pathological outcomes. Without a cultural framework, unique factors that may contribute to the adjustment and resiliency of these individuals may be overlooked. To establish such framework, we drew from indigenous psychology and proposed a Taiwanese International Bicultural Model with three dimensions: priority, locus of control, and support systems. Several culturally relevant concepts (i.e., group harmony, forbearance, go with the flow, reframing, ren-qing, and mien-tzu) that are particularly relevant to adjustment among this population fell into these three dimensions. Implications for research and practice are described in the following sections.

Implications for Research

Most studies on Taiwanese international students were conducted in the 1990s. Since the 2000s, there has been a trend to aggregate Taiwanese international students with students from China and Hong Kong under the "ethnically Chinese" umbrella. Given the contextual differences, it is imperative for future studies to separate the populations to better understand the unique adjustment experiences for these subgroups. It is also important to acknowledge that this chapter does not provide an exhaustive list of culturally-relevant concepts but focuses more on major psychological factors that may be associated with adjustment, resilience, and coping. The Taiwanese International Bicultural Model postulated in this chapter is a helpful framework when exploring how other concepts (e.g., hierarchy, respect) may be relevant to Taiwanese international students' cross-national journey and their psychological adjustment. As well, researchers may consider utilizing the model as a foundation for exploring identity development (e.g., racial identity, nationality) in the U.S. context to understand how individuals adopt new identities while negotiating to keep or adjust existing identities and values. Lastly, we expect this model to help bridge the gap between the Taiwanese and U.S. literature on the adjustment among Taiwanese international students. Researchers are encouraged to utilize this model as a framework for empirical studies, both qualitatively and quantitatively, to better understand how the three dimensions in the model and cultural concepts can act as moderating or mediating factors between predictors and psychological outcomes. It is also important to note that there are individual differences between Taiwanese individuals and that they may not all share the same worldview on mental health or mental illness and how it pertains to treatment (余德慧, 1998 [Yu, 1998]). For example, Yu (1998) provides an illustration of three members of the same Taiwanese family on how their adoption of different religions and cultural values impact their interpretation of psychosis and decision to seek treatment from Western or Eastern medicine.

In sum, it is important to differentiate Taiwanese from Chinese samples in empirical studies due to the nuanced cultural differences between these groups. Researchers who are interested in studying the experiences of Taiwanese international students may seek out cultural sensitivity training in order to avoid condoning stereotypes or perpetrating acts of microaggressions during interviews or survey construction. To avoid overgeneralization, when a Taiwanese international student sample is combined with other Asian ethnic groups, it should be addressed as a limitation in research.

Implications for Practice

Several practical implications may be derived from the three dimensions of the Taiwanese International Bicultural Model proposed in this chapter. Educators or mental health practitioners may use a more proactive approach to engage Taiwanese international students in classrooms or mental health services. First, regarding the priority dimension, it may be helpful for instructors to attend to classroom management in which cross-cultural communication is incorporated into the curriculum to better facilitate cross-cultural and multicultural understanding among students from various backgrounds. For example, given that Taiwanese international students may give priority to others' opinions over their own, instructors may consider inviting Taiwanese international students to join in on class discussions or asking for their input. Instructors may also consider inviting Taiwanese international students to share information about topics that may be viewed differently in the Taiwanese context. In addition, it may be helpful for instructors to be more flexible with the platform of discussion, such as allowing students to have options on how to participate in class (e.g., online versus in-person). For mental health practitioners, it may be useful to help students learn the ways to balance the needs of the self with those of others (e.g., parents, instructors, peers). Clinicians may discuss the costs and consequences of different choices with students to help them recognize their own needs and reduce the potential guilt when prioritizing themselves over others.

In regards to the locus of control, it would be beneficial for those working with Taiwanese international students to understand their worldview without judgment, as many may interpret individuals who hold an external locus of control as "lazy." Practitioners may empower students by identifying the degree to which they have control to maximize their personal strengths. In other words, working with students on recognizing what aspects in their lives they feel that they have control over, rather than generalizing the belief that everything is outside of their control. For example, clinicians may invite students to share what makes them feel in control and how they can apply past successes to other areas of their lives. Additionally, it is important for practitioners to keep in mind the balance between empowerment and respecting the degree to which individuals adhere to the belief of external locus of control. In practice, instead of solely focusing on results or interpreting external locus of control behaviors as "avoidance," clinicians may consider working with students on identifying what was learned throughout the process. Nevertheless, practitioners may also need to challenge individuals to take on personal responsibilities when appropriate. For instance, practitioners may provide psychoeducation to students on the decision-making process by breaking down the factors and identifying the pieces that they are in charge of, and the actions they can take in order to be an active participant in their own narratives.

With respect to support systems dimension, it is important to consider the elements that impact Taiwanese students' decision-making process to seeking help. When considering whether to seek support from a friend or a professional, scholars found that Taiwanese international students take into account the following factors: consideration of the familiarity with friends, whether there is a possibility of disrupting mien-tzu with friends, and the credibility of the professional (韓桂香、李美枝, 2008 [Han & Li, 2008]). Considering these elements, for administrators, it may be useful to increase the accessibility and credibility of professionals (e.g., mental health counselors) as resources for Taiwanese international students. For instance, professionals may consider outreach events where students have the opportunity to familiarize themselves with the staff and resources available. Likewise, to overcome the stigma of seeking counseling, Li, Wong, and Toth

(2013) suggested counseling centers to focus on academic-related issues in order to attract Asian international students to their services, which may also decrease the possibility of losing mien-tzu. Practitioners may also consider providing support groups for Taiwanese international students given that they are more likely to seek help from their social capital. It may also be important to emphasize the prepaid nature of resources on-campus in order to decrease the feelings of indebtedness towards professionals while increasing students' desire to seek help from such resources.

Given the complicated historical context and current political climate between Taiwan and China, Taiwanese international students may experience discomfort, oppression, and other identity-related distress on a regular basis. For example, being perceived and labeled as "Chinese" frequently by their peers, instructors, and administrative staff due to similarities with Chinese from Mainland China (e.g., Mandarin-speakers, celebrating the same festivals and traditional events). To establish a trustworthy relationship, clinicians can demonstrate curiosity towards Taiwanese culture, invite students to discuss the differences between Taiwan and China and their self-identification. After a better understanding of how Taiwanese international students position themselves in the larger context (e.g., Taiwan, the U.S., internationally), practitioners can then further work with students on processing emotions (e.g., anger, anxiety, confusion) and developing appropriate coping strategies regarding the stress related to their experiences. While leading groups consisting both Taiwanese and Chinese members, group facilitators may need to be mindful of potential power differences and avoid generalizing the experiences of Chinese participants' experience to those of Taiwanese members. Facilitators would also need to be sensitive to avoid replicating the dynamics of the political climate in the group (e.g., Chinese participants silencing Taiwanese by invalidating their citizenship) while considering the three dimensions in the Taiwanese International Bicultural Model to address the issues in a culturally congruent matter.

In sum, the Taiwanese International Bicultural Model model can be used as a practical tool to guide educators and mental health practitioners working with Taiwanese international students to assess where students fall under each dimension. It is important to recognize that there are individual differences in regards to how students prioritize oneself versus others, their perception of locus of control, and utilization of support systems. Thus, it may be helpful for practitioners to ask students to self-identify where they believe they are on each dimension and where they would like themselves to be while reminding them that the level of adherence to each dimension is fluid and not fixed.

REFERENCES

Ang, S., Van Dyne, L., Koh, C., Ng, K. Y., Templer, K. J., Tay, C., & Chandrasekar, N. A. (2007). Cultural intelligence: Its measurement and effects on cultural judgment and decision making, cultural adaptation, and task performance. *Management and Organization Review, 3*, 335–371. doi:10.1111/j.1740-8784.2007.00082.x.

Becker, G. S. (1964). *Human capital: A theoretical and empirical analysis with special reference to education.* New York, NY: National Bureau of Economic Research.

Lee, A. Y.-P., Bei, L., & DeVaney, S. A. (2007). Acculturation experiences of Taiwanese students during exchanges in the United States. *Journal of Family and Consumer Sciences, 99*, 56-61.

Bian, Y. J. (2001). Guanxi Capital and Social Eating: Theoretical Models and Empirical Analyses. In N. Lin, K. Cook and R.S. Burt (Eds.), *Social Capital: Theory and Research* (pp. 275–295). New York, NY: Aldine de Gruyter.

Bochner, S., Furnham, A., & Ward, C. (2001). *The psychology of culture shock* (2nd ed). Hove, East Sussex: Routledge.

Brislin, R. W. (1980). In H. C. Triandis & J. W. Berry (Eds.), *Translation and content analysis of oral and written materials. Handbook of cross-cultural psychology* (Vol. 2, pp. 389-444). Boston, MA: Allyn & Bacon.

Central Intelligence Agency (2019). *The world factbook. East Asian/Southeast Asia: Taiwan.* Retrieved from https://www.cia.gov/library/publications/the-world-factbook/geos/tw.html.

Chan, E. (2002). Beyond pedagogy: Language and identity in post-colonial Hong Kong. British *Journal of Sociology of Education, 23*, 271-285. doi:10.1080.01425690220137756.

Chang, M. J., Denson, N., Sáenz, V., & Misa, K. (2005). The educational benefits of sustaining cross-racial interaction among undergraduates. *Center for Studies in Higher Education.* UC Berkeley: Center for Studies in Higher Education. Retrieved from: http://escholarship.org/uc/item/2d83s4q0.

Chataway, C. J., & Berry, J. W. (1989). Acculturation experiences, appraisal, coping, and adaptation: A comparison of Hong Kong Chinese, French, and English students in Canada. *Canadian Journal of Behavioral Science/Revue Canadienne Des Sciences Du Comportement, 21*, 295-309. doi:10.1037/h0079820.

Chen, H.-L. (2017). *Taiwanese/Chinese identification trend distribution in Taiwan (1992/06-2017/06).* Election Study Center National Chengchi University. Retrieved from http://esc.nccu.edu.tw/course/news.php?Sn=166.

Chen, Y. -A. (2013). *A study on Taiwanese international students and Taiwanese American students: The interface between naming and identity* (Unpublished master's thesis). San José State University, San José, CA.

Cortina, L. M. (2004). Hispanic perspectives on sexual harassment and social support. *Personality and Social Psychology Bulletin, 30*, 570–584. doi:10.1177/0146167203262854.

Dao, T. K., Lee, D., & Chang, H. L. (2007). Acculturation level, perceived English fluency, perceived social support level, and depression among Taiwanese international students. *College Student Journal, 41*, 287-295.

Department of Statistics (2018). *Population statistics.* Retrieved from https://www.moi.gov.tw/stat/chart.aspx

Diener, E., Emmons, R. A., Larsen, R. J., & Griffin, S. (1985). The Satisfaction With Life Scale. *Journal of Personality Assessment, 49*, 71–75. doi:10.1207/s15327752jpa4901_13.

Dipeolu, A., Kang, J., & Cooper, C. (2007). Support group for international students: a counseling center's experience. *Journal of College Student Psychotherapy, 22*, 63–74. doi:10.1300/J035v22n01_05.

Earley, P. C., & Ang, S. (2003). *Cultural intelligence: Individual interactions across cultures*. Pala Alto, CA: Stanford University Press.

Edmondson, R. (2009). *Negotiations of Taiwan's identity among generations of liuxuesheng (overseas students) and Taiwanese Americans* (Unpublished doctoral dissertation). Michigan State University, East Lansing, MI.

Feng, H. (2015). Embracing cultural similarities and bridging differences in supportive communication. *Journal of Asian Pacific Communication*, special issue, 22-41.

Greenberg, M. S. (1980). A theory of indebtedness. In K. Gergen, M. Greenberg, & R. Wills (Eds.), *Social exchange: Advances in theory and research* (pp. 3-26). New York: Plenum.

Gurin, P., Dey, E., Hurtado, S., & Gurin, G. (2002). Diversity and higher education: Theory and impact on educational outcomes. *Harvard Educational Review, 72*, 330-366. doi:10.17763/haer.72.3.01151786u134n051.

Hammer, M. R., Bennett, M. J., & Wisemer, R. (2003). Measuring intercultural sensitivity: The Intercultural Development Inventory. *International Journal of Intercultural Relations, 27*, 421-443. doi:10.1016/S0147-1767(03)00032-4.

Heggins, W. J., & Jackson, J. F. L. (2003). Understanding the collegiate experience for Asian international students at a Midwestern research university. *College Student Journal, 37*, 379-391.

Heppner, P. P., Wang, K. T., Heppner, M. J., & Wang, L. F. (2012). From cultural encapsulation to cultural competence: The cross-national cultural competence model. In N. A. Fouad, J. A. Carter, & L. M. Subich (EDs.), *APA handbook of counseling psychology: Vol. 2. Practice, interventions, and applications* (pp. 433-471). Washington, DC: American Psychological Association. doi:10.1037/13755-018.

Herskovits, M. J. (1948). The contribution of Afroamerican studies to Africanist research. *American Anthropologist, 50,* 1–10. doi:10.1525/aa.1948.50.1.02a00020.

Hsu, C. F. (2007), Cross-cultural comparison of communication orientations between Americans and Taiwanese. *Communication Quarterly, 55,* 359-74.

Hsu, K. Y., Wang, D. F., & Yang, K. S. (2001). Differences between Taiwanese and Mainland Chinese on Chinese Basic Personality Dimensions: A preliminary study. *Indigenous Psychological Research in Chinese Society, 16,* 185-224. doi:10.6254/16.185.

Hu, H. (1944). The Chinese concepts of "face". *American Anthropologist, 46,* 45-64. doi:10.1525/aa.1944.46.1.02a00040.

Huang, A. (2014*). In search of sojourners' ethnic identity development: Taiwanese international doctoral students in the United States* (Unpublished doctoral dissertation). Northern Illinois University, Dekalb, IL.

Huang, T. L. (2016, August 14). Taiwanese in US demand ethnicity option in census. *Taipei Times.* Retrieved from http://www.taipeitimes.com/News/taiwan/archives/2016/08/14/2003653101.

Huang, Y. W. (2009). *Listening to their voices: An in-depth study of language anxiety and cultural adjustment among Taiwanese graduate students in the United States* (Unpublished doctoral dissertation). Indiana University of Pennsylvania, Indiana, PA.

Hwang, K. K. (1977). The patterns of coping strategies in a Chinese society. *Acta Psychologica Taiwanica, 19,* 61–73.

Hwang, W. C. (2006). The psychotherapy adaptation and modification framework: Application to Asian Americans. *American Psychologist, 61,* 702–715. doi:10.1037/0003-066X.61.7.702.

Institute of International Education. (2010). *International student totals by place of origin, 2008/09-2009/10.* Retrieved from https://www.iie.org/Research-and-Insights/Open-Doors/Data/International-Students/Leading-Places-of-Origin/2009-10.

Institute of International Education. (2016). *International Student Totals by Place of Origin, 2014/15- 2015/16.* Retrieved from https://

www.iie.org/Research-and-Insights/Open-Doors/Data/International-Students/Leading-Places-of-Origin/2015-16.

Institute of International Education. (2017a). *Fast-facts 2016. Open doors report on international educational exchange.* Retrieved from https://www.iie.org/-/media/Files/Corporate/Open-Doors/Fast-Facts/Fast-Facts-2016.ashx?la=en&hash=9E918FD13976 8E1631E06A3C280D8A9F2F22BBE1

Institute of International Education. (2017b). *Open doors data: Fact sheets by country 2016.* Retrieved from https://p.widencdn.net/xpzaae/Open-Doors-2017-Country-Sheets-Taiwan.

Institute of International Education. (2018). *Open door data: International student totals by place of origin.* Retrieved from https://www.iie.org/Research-and-Insights/Open-Doors/Data/International-Students/Places-of-Origin.

Kao, S.-F. (2013). Follow the situational rules or your heart? Individual differences in behavior under critical situations among Taiwanese. *Indigenous Psychological Research in Chinese Society, 40,* 3-44. doi:10.6254/2013.40.3.

Keyes, C. L. M. (2005). Mental illness and/or mental health? Investigating Axioms of the complete state model of health. *Journal of Consulting & Clinical Psychology, 73,* 539-548. doi:10.1037/0022-006X.73.3.539.

King, A. Y. S., & Myers, J. T. (1977). *Shame as an incomplete conception of Chinese culture: A study of face.* Hong Kong: Social Research Center.

Lin, C.-Y. (2004). *Taiwanese students in a U.S. university: Expectations, beliefs, values, and attitudes about learning and teaching* (Unpublished doctoral dissertation). Pennsylvania State University, State College, PA.

LaFromboise, T., Coleman, H. L. K., & Gerton, J. (1993). Psychological impact of biculturalism: Evidence and theory. *Psychological Bulletin, 3,* 395-412. doi:0033-2909.114.3.395.

Li, P., Wong, Y., & Toth, P. (2013). Asian international students' willingness to seek counseling: A mixed-methods study. *International Journal for the Advancement of Counselling, 35,* 1-15. doi:s10447-012-9163-7.

Lin, Y. C., Huang, C. L., & Lee, Y. C. (2011). Stepping backward or moving forward: Flexibility of situated forbearance and psychological adjustment. *Indigenous Psychological Research in Chinese Society, 35,* 57-100. doi:10.6254/2011.35.57.

Lin, Y. N. (2017). Subjective wellbeing experiences of Taiwanese university students. *Education, 137,* 333-343.

Lu, L. (2003). Defining the self-other relation: The emergence of composite self. *Indigenous Psychology Research in Chinese Societies, 20,* 139-207. doi:10.6254/2003.20.139.

Mitchell, S. L., Greenwood, A. K., & Guglielmi, M. C. (2007). Utilization of counseling services: comparing international students and U.S. college students. *Journal of College Counseling, 10,* 117–129. doi:j.2161-1882.2007.tb00012.x.

Mizuno, H., & Ishikuma, T. (1999). Help-seeking preferences and help-seeking behaviors: An overview of studies. *The Japanese Journal of Educational Psychology, 47,* 530–539. doi:10.5926/jjep1953.47.4_530.

Mojaverian, T., Hashimoto, T., & Kim, H. S. (2012). Cultural differences in professional help seeking: A comparison of Japan and the U.S. *Frontiers in Psychology, 3,* 615. doi:10.3389/fpsyg.2012.00615.

Morgan, S. (2019, January 21). Taiwan rejects 'one-China principle' as support for independence rises: poll. *Taiwan News.* Retrieved from https://www.taiwannews.com.tw/en/news/3622244.

NAFSA: Association of International Educators. (2018). *The United States of America: Benefits from international students.* Retrieved from http://www.nafsa.org/Policy_and_Advocacy/Policy_Resources/Policy_Trends_and_Data/NAFSA_International_Student_Economic_Value_Tool/.

Nilsson, J. E., Berkel, L. A., Flores, L. Y., & Lucas, M. S. (2004). Utilization rate and presenting concerns of international students at a university counseling center: Implications for Outreach Programming. *Journal of College Student Psychotherapy, 19,* 49-59. doi:10.1300/J035v19n02_05.

Oyserman, D., Coon, H. M., & Kemmelmeier, M. (2002). Rethinking individualism and collectivism: Evaluation of theoretical assumptions and meta-analyses. *Psychological Bulletin, 128,* 3–72. doi:10.1037/0033-2909.128.1.3.

Pappamihiel, N. E. (2002). English as a second language students and English language anxiety: Issues in the mainstream classroom. *Research in the Teaching of English, 36*, 327-355.

Patton, M. Q. (2002). *Qualitative research & evaluation methods* (3rd ed.). Thousand Oaks, CA: Sage.

Periasamy, S., & Ashby, J. S. (2002). Multidimensional perfectionism and locus of control: Adaptive vs. maladaptive perfectionism. *Journal of College Student Psychotherapy, 17*, 75-86. doi:10.1300/J035v17n02_06.

Pham, H. (2013). Oceans crossing: Factors contributing to the social and academic integration of Korean, Malaysian, and Taiwanese international undergraduate students at a research university (Unpublished doctoral dissertation). Michigan State University, East Lansing, MI.

Ross, C. E., & Mirowsky, J. (1989). Explaining the social patterns of depression: Control and problem-solving--or support and talking? *Journal of Health and Social Behavior, 30*, 206-219.

Schmitt, M. T., Spears, R., & Branscombe, N. R. (2003). Constructing a minority group identity out of shared rejection: The case of international students. *European Journal of Social Psychology, 33*, 1-12. doi:10.1002/ejsp.131.

Shek, D. T. (1998). Help-seeking patterns of Chinese parents in Hong Kong. *Asia Pacific Journal of Social Work, 8*, 106–119. doi:10.1080/21650993.1998.9755782.

Shenkar, O. (2001). Cultural distance revisited: Towards a more rigorous conceptualization and measurement of cultural differences. *Journal of International Business Studies, 32*, 519-535. doi:10.1057/palgrave.jibs.8490982.

Shih, S. F., & Brown, C. (2000). Taiwanese international students: Acculturation level and vocational identity. *Journal of Career Development, 27*, 35-47. doi:10.1177/089484530002700103.

Shin, J. Y. (2002). Social support for families of children with mental retardation: Comparison between Korea and the United States. *Mental*

Retardation, 40, 103-118. doi:10.1352/0047-6765(2002)040<0103: SSFFOC>2.0.CO;2.

Sue, D. W., & Sue, D. (2015). *Counseling the culturally diverse* (6th ed.). Hoboken, NJ: John Wiley & Sons.

Swagler, M. A., & Ellis, M. V. (2003). Crossing the distance: Adjustment of Taiwanese graduate students in the United States. *Journal of Counseling Psychology, 50*, 420-437. doi:10.1037/0022-0167.50.4.420.

Tone, H. (2002). Chinese national character and pursuit of universe-human synchronization. *Indigenous Psychological Research in Chinese Societies, 17*, 245-275. doi:10.6254/2002.17.245.

Triandis, H. C. (1995). *Individualism & collectivism.* Boulder, CO: Westview Press.

Wang, C. C. D. C., & Mallinckrodt, B. (2006). Acculturation, attachment, and psychosocial adjustment of Chinese/Taiwanese international students. *Journal of Counseling Psychology, 53*, 422-433. doi:10.1037/0022-0167.53.4.422.

Wang, L., Wang, K. T., Heppner, P. P., & Chuang, C.-C. (2016). Cross-national cultural competency among Taiwanese international students. *Journal of Diversity in Higher Education.* Advance online publication (http://psycnet.apa.org/psycinfo/2016-12804-001/). doi:10.1037/dhe0000020.

Wei, M., Heppner, P. P., Mallen, M. J., Ku, T. Y., Liao, K. Y. H., & Wu, T. F. (2007). Acculturative stress, perfectionism, years in the United States, and depression among Chinese international students. *Journal of Counseling Psychology, 54*, 385-394. doi:10.1037/0022-0167.54.4.385.

Wu, C. Y. (2014). *Qualitative study of Taiwanese students studying abroad: Social interactions, navigating US culture, and experiences learning English language* (Unpublished doctoral dissertation). Wayne State University, Detroit, MI.

Yan, M. C., & Lam, C. M. (2009). Intersecting social capital and Chinese culture: Implications for services assisting unemployed youths. *International Social Work, 52*, 195-207. doi:10.1177/0020872808099730.

Yang, K. S., & Lu, L. (2005). Social- and individual-oriented self-actualizers: Conceptual analysis and empirical assessment of their psychological characteristics. *Indigenous Psychological Research in Chinese Societies, 23*, 71-143.

Yang, Y. T. T. (2010). *Stress, coping, and psychological well-being: Comparison among American and Asian international graduates from Taiwan, China, and South Korea* (Unpublished doctoral dissertation). University of Kansas, Lawrence, KS.

Ying, Y. W. (2005). Variation in acculturative stressors over time: A study of Taiwanese students in the United States. *International Journal of Intercultural Relations, 29*, 59-71. doi:10.1016/j.ijintrel.2005.04.003.

Ying, Y. W., & Han, M. (2006). The contribution of personality, acculturative stressors, and social affiliation to adjustment: A longitudinal study of Taiwanese students in the United States. *International Journal of Intercultural Relations, 30*, 623-635. doi:10.1016/j.ijintrel.2006.02.001.

Ying, Y. W., & Han, M. (2008). Variation in the prediction of cross-cultural adjustment by ethnic density: A longitudinal study of Taiwanese students in the United States. *College Student Journal, 42*, 1075-1086.

余德慧（1998）. 生活受苦經驗的心理病理：本土文化的探索. **本土心理學研究**, [Yu, D.-H. (1998). The painful life experiences of psychopathology: Exploration of indigenous culture. *Indigenous Psychological Research in Chinese Societies*] 10, 69-115. doi:10.6254/1998.12.69.*

林楠森(2007).民進黨"四大天王"黨內初選辯論.取自 BBC 中文網: 年 4 月 14 日. [Lin, S.-N. (2007, April 14). *Democratic Progress Party's primary debate*] Retrieved from http://news.bbc.co.uk/chinese/trad/hi/newsid_6550000/newsid_6555300/6555363.stm, 2007.*

林宜旻（2004）. **受助者負債感之內涵與其前因後果之探討──以組織內的受助事件為例**. 政治大學心理學研究所，未發表之博士論文. [Lin, Y. M. (2004). *The connotations of the sense of indebtedness of the recipient and its causes: From a within-systems example*. (Unpublished doctoral dissertation). National Chengchi University, Taipei, Taiwan.]*

林倖妃 (2017). 2017《天下》國情調查I：39歲, 民意的斷裂點. 取自天下雜誌網站: Retrieved from: http://www.cw.com.tw/article/article.action?id=5080204, 2017, 年1月3日. [Lin, H.-F. (2017, January 3). 2017 Common Wealth National Survey I: 39 years old, the breaking point of public opinion].*

梁明義、王文音 (2009). 台灣半世紀以來快速經濟發展的回顧與省思. 載於林建甫 (主編): 金融投資與經濟發展: 紀念梁國樹教授第六屆學術研討會論文集 （127-130. 國立台灣大學經濟學系. [Liang, M.-Y., & Wang, W.-Y. (2009). A review and reflection of Taiwan's rapid enconomic growth in the last half century. In Chien-Fu Li (Ed.), *Financial investment and economic development: The 6th annual Dr. Liang Kuo-Shu Conference papers* (pp. 127-130). Department of Finance, National Taiwan University.]*

陸洛 (2011. 現代華人的雙文化自我與雙重陷落. **本土心理學研究**, 36, 155-168. doi:10.6254/2011.36.155 [Lu, L. (2011). The contemporary Chinese bi-cultural self and its double jeopardy. *Indigenous Psychological Research in Chinese Societies, 36,* 155-168].

楊國樞 (1999). 中國人之性格知覺向度的系統性研究. 國立台灣大學心理學系, 未發表之論文. [Yang, K.-S. (1999). *Systematic study of perception of Chinese personality.* (Unpublished doctoral dissertation). National Taiwan University, Taipei, Taiwan.]

鄭如雲 (2007). **亞太國家留學政策之研究**. 國立臺灣科技大學技術及職業教育研究所, 未發表之博士論文. [Cheng, J.-Y. (2007). *A Study on overseas education policies of Asia-Pacific countries.* (Unpublished Master's thesis). National Taiwan University of Science and Technology, Taipei, Taiwan.]

鄭伯壎 (1999). 華人人關係研究的困境與出路. **本土心理學研究**, 12, 203-214. doi:10.6524/1999.12.203 [Cheng, B.-S. (1999). The difficulties and solutions of studying interpersonal relationships among Chinese. *Indigenous Psychological Research in Chinese Societies, 12,* 203-214. doi:10.6524/1999.12.203]*

賴澤涵 (2013). 台灣人才之培育 — 兼談留學政策問題. **台灣教育,** 684, 14-16. [Lai, Y.-H. (2013). The cultivation of talents in Taiwan and the policies of study abroad. *Taiwan Education Review, 684,* 14-16.]*

戴肇洋 (2005). **出國留學人數降低問題及因應對策** (61-65). 臺北: 行政院研究發展考核委員會. 取自國家發展委員會網站: https://www.ndc.gov.tw/News_Content.aspx?n=E4F9C91CF6EA4EC4&sms=4506D295372B40FB&s=637DA503B764E7AC, 2017 年 8 月 11 日。[Dai, C.-Y. (2005). *The solutions for the decrease in students studying abroad.* Research, Development, and Evulation Commission, Taipei City Government (pp. 61-65). Retrieved from https://www.ndc.gov.tw/News_Content.aspx?n=E4F9C91CF6EA4EC4&sms=4506D295372B40FB&s=637DA503B764E7AC]*

韓貴香 (2003). 自我概念差異、不同生活向度滿足與正、負向情感感受之關係—以台灣女性幼教老師為例. **中華心理衛生學刊**, 16, 1-22. [Han, K.-H. (2003). The affective consequences of different self-construals and satisfaction with different life-domains-A study of Taiwanese female teachers in kindergarten. *Mental Health Taiwan, 16,* 1-22.]

韓貴香、李美枝 (2011). 大我的道德臉面受威脅對華人選擇求助對象的影響. **本土心理學研究**, 36, 3-32. doi:10.6254/2011.36.3.LCH [Han, K.-H., & Li, M.-C. (2011). The effect of the big self and moral face on the choice of helpers in a Confucian society. *Indigenous Psychological Research in Chinese Societies, 36,* 3-32. doi:10.6254/2011.36.3.LCH]

*Translated by the authors due to reference being available only in Traditional Chinese.

Chapter 2

INTEGRATED PERSPECTIVES ON ACADEMIC, SOCIAL AND PSYCHOLOGICAL ADJUSTMENT AMONG INTERNATIONAL STUDENTS

Sarifah Nurhanum Syed Sahuri[1] and Rachel Wilson[2]

[1]Faculty of Major Language Studies,
Islamic Science University of Malaysia, Nilai, Malaysia
[2]Sydney School of Education and Social Work,
Faculty of Arts and Social Science, The University of Sydney,
Sydney, Australia

ABSTRACT

The wellbeing of international students is central to the social good and economic productivity of international education across higher education institutions. As international students are the largest shareholder in the international education industry, their perspectives and interests need to be understood and protected. In particular, the challenges of adjusting to new circumstances in their host countries need to be understood so that programs can more fully support students. Substantial research maps out these challenges. However, research has tended to focus on psychological, social and academic adjustment as separate domains. We present an argument for integrating these perspectives; and we highlight the interrelation between these domains in empirical data collected using a new, integrated measure of students' academic, social and psychological adjustment among one international student population sample. We argue that sensitive exploration and surveying of these three inter-related domains of adjustment among specific sub-groups of international students, enables deeper understanding and empathy to be translated into supportive institutional practice that can be directly customised to those students' specific needs. Such an approach can contribute to more culturally sensitive, but holistically focussed, understanding of students, enabling them to flourish.

Keywords: international student, academic adjustment, social adjustment, psychological adjustment

INTRODUCTION

The globalization of higher education has initiated international student mobility around the world [1]. This phenomenon [2] reformed the distribution of the international student population and market as well as the direction of research on this group [3]. More than five million tertiary students are currently studying outside their nation of citizenship [4]. The international education database shows a steady increase in the number of foreign or international students enrolled in various levels of degree programs from 2 million in 1998 to 5 million in 2016 across 38 countries around the world [4].

The growth of the international student population has been evident for Western countries like United States, United Kingdom, Australia, and more recently, Luxembourg and Switzerland [5]. These countries have been the major players in the international education market for several decades [1]. Most international students have a strong determination to study overseas, in particular at the "world class universities" [6] in Western countries [7]. They believe that a degree from a prestigious institution of English speaking country will lift the quality of their life in the future [8].

The sophistication of the international education market has a powerful impact on many aspects of each country involved. This market has shaped governments' and universities' policy, funding, and regulations, in order to sustain the benefits and revenue from international student enrolments [9]. National strategies, such as increasing their universities' rankings or providing free education, are also used to increase international student numbers [10]. Obtaining recognition and ranking from a higher education research agency such as Times Higher Education and Higher Education Network [11] has encouraged international students to study in particular countries, especially the United States and United Kingdom, as their universities have been listed as having leading or excellent universities in the world rankings.

Behind the globalisation phenomenon, international student mobility has produced many stories of personal international student adjustment experiences. The greater part of the literature on international students' adjustment experiences in Western countries comes from Australia, the United States, United Kingdom, and New Zealand [12]. However, these personal experiences are largely unexamined and rarely documented in culturally sensitive ways [13]. International students, as a group, are often labelled as a vulnerable or undermined and at-risk group [14]. They are exposed to difficulties and challenges while adjusting to new living and studying environments. Thus, many scholars have relocated their focus and efforts to studying the international student adjustment experience [15, 16, 13, 17, 18, 19, 20, 21].

The well-established concept of adjustment includes a focus on the relationship between the sociocultural and psychological domains [22, 23]. However, the academic adjustment aspect has not been directly integrated into these perspectives. In previous research, sociocultural and psychological domains of adjustment have been typically treated as distinctive and separate to academic adjustment; the latter which may [24, 25] or may not [26, 27, 28] have been in such studies. The idea of combining these three domains should be seen as positive and holistic, with the potential to increase the impact of studying the relationship between the domains, and to provide a more comprehensive account of the process of adaptation of international students.

INTERNATIONAL STUDENT'S ADJUSTMENT TO THEIR HOST COUNTRY

International students' experience and satisfaction have become an imperative agenda for universities in Australia, where our research is set [9]. In order to sustain international student mobility to Australia, higher education institutions have increased the quality of their customer service to strengthen their reputation as a "world class" universities. Studies of international student satisfaction have been conducted at national [29, 30] and state levels [31]. The International Student Barometer (ISB) is used to measure five aspects: learning experience, support services, arrival experiences (limited to first-year students), living experience, and overall experience. The Australian government has come out with a policy blueprint for international education, to guide the universities in giving the best service to international students.

Most of the studies on the international student adjustment experience use three concepts or terms: acculturation, adjustment, and adaptation. In synthesis, the adjustment concept has become the central focus of the literature, but it retains strong association with the to the acculturation and adaptation concepts [32, 33, 34, 35].

Most of the studies of the international student adjustment experience can be classified according to focus on one or more of three domains: academic, sociocultural, and psychological adjustment. Each domain has a particular effect on the international student adjustment experience. In this section, the discussion of each domain outlines the issues, problems, or strategies arising during adjustment.

Academic Adjustment

The main purpose of studying abroad is to gain an academic or professional certificate in a particular field of study from the university or college. Previous studies have found that international students are struggling to adapt to their new academic environment because of differences in learning and teaching culture and values between the home and host countries, which have created some difficulties for these international students [36]. One of the major problems experienced by international students is in English skills, especially regarding their ability in writing, reading, and speaking. The student failure to use English language as a medium of learning affects student academic performance. Examining this academic aspect, previous studies have focused on international students' lack of academic skills: this refers to students' general skills in managing their study in the classroom and transitioning into the Western teaching and learning style [37, 38, 39]. Unsupportive classmates and lecturers, as well as low quality environment and experience of learning have also been examined [40, 41]. A multitude of studies have documented the many factors that contribute to international students' successful academic adjustment, such as self-regulation and motivation [42, 43]. Previous studies also highlight how study management techniques, learning preparation, and maximal class participation will help international students to adapt to the different teaching and learning culture [44, 45, 46]. International students with high self-efficacy and communication skills, for example, have also increased chances to perform well in the academic area [47, 15, 48]. Also, positive learning experiences, such as with high quality and well-organised courses and knowledgeable academic staff, also help them to overcome their adjustment problems in the university [49, 50, 51, 46].

Social Adjustment

Sociocultural challenges and problems emanate from the cultural distance between the international students' home country and the host country; this distance is a measure of the cultural differences in values, behaviours and lifestyles [52]. The origin culture of international students that was nurtured by parents and their communities, while growing up in their home country, impacts upon their perceptions, views, and behaviours towards the different culture of the host country. The difference between these two cultures can be called a cultural distance [53]. Previous studies have argued that international students might struggle to adjust to their new environment if the cultural distance between the home and host country culture is too large [54]. In addition, lack of knowledge in relation to the host country culture, difficulties in practicing Islam, and prejudice and discrimination, especially for female students [55] are documented social and cultural issues among students [56].

International students obviously experience difficulties in mixing with the new community as the result of such cultural distance [46, 57]. In this context, again, English language skills, such as writing, reading, listening and speaking, moderate the impact of cultural distance; and challenges with these contribute to sociocultural problems [48, 58]. These challenges are such that students often avoid communication with the host country students or other international students, and to prefer to strengthen their relationships with students of the same nationality [59]. As a result, international students tend to experience less social interaction and frequently have only a small number of local friends at the university. This pattern of friendship may obstruct them from creating quality friendships with other students, especially those from different national groups [60].

In addition, research has highlighted the ways in which sociocultural adjustment has an effect on international student satisfaction and happiness in their new home [46]. For example, many international students feel satisfied with the locals' response and acceptance towards their social presence in the community, even though some students have also experienced discrimination or racism because of cultural and religious differences [56, 61]. Previous studies also have found that sociocultural problems have a significant effect on psychological adjustment [62, 63], [23]. Research by Terry [64] reports that international students have emotional difficulties when they perceive their origin culture as being considered to be of low status by the host country. Other studies have reported that international students feel disturbed with their social status in the new environment [65] and are at increased risk of psychological isolation [13].

Previous studies indicate that there are several strategies in academic adjustment which also aid in students' sociocultural adjustment; such as students' travel preparation, level of active participation, self-efficacy, communication, and social support [40]. In the sociocultural context, students' preparatory understanding of the host country culture, and efforts toward maximum participation in the society, are effective strategies for adaptation to the host country. International students with high cultural self-efficacy are more likely have regular communication, interaction with the host society and strong social support systems; and this impacts positively in terms of adaption to the different and new culture [66, 67]. It follows that strong efforts by locals to identify, meet and engage with international students will maximise the international students' adjustment experience. Therefore, it is important for universities and administrators to help and encourage international students to get involved in university activities. Student participation in community activities, beyond the university, will also help them to have a better adjustment experience [68].

Psychological Adjustment

In the early phase of adjustment, international students usually feel excited and happy during their arrival in the new place [69]. However, after several weeks, some of them start to experience culture shock due to the significant cultural differences, that can precipitate emotional and psychological problems. In addition, dysfunctional coping strategies can contribute to their level of stress [70].

In terms of emotional well-being, students' experience of loneliness, homesickness and isolation in the early stage of adjustment often makes them feel nervous, scared, frustrated, anxious, embarrassed and uncertain, till at some point they become overwhelmed and depressed with all these negative emotions [72] [73]. These three issues (loneliness, homesickness and isolation) were found to have a strong mutual relationship and have tended to be discussed together in the literature on international students' psychological adjustment [74, 41, 56]. To compound these challenges, most of the international students, particularly first year international undergraduate students, also worry about financial matters and show stress symptoms at a moderate level, with some in the severe category. They also reported high levels of diarrhoea, poor memory, and depression [37]. Less commonly some international students have experienced psychological problems such as an obsessive-compulsive disorder because of their perfectionist attitude and determination to achieve excellent results in their studies [75]. Mori reviews the psychological experiences of international students and argues that, despite a litany of challenges and vulnerabilities, international students remained impoverished regarding mental health services [76].

Acculturative stress has a negative impact on psychological adjustment but some students show resilience. Researchers have argued that there are three factors that influence psychological adjustment: personal growth initiative, hardiness, and universal-diverse orientation [77]. However, their data analysis suggests that only students with high personal growth initiative have a strong positive psychological adjustment experience, compared to hardiness and universal-diverse orientation. In addition, hope and optimism are two elements of positive psychology that have been found to help students to control or increase their psychological adjustment [28]. In this study, correlation analysis indicated that maladaptive coping strategies and acculturative stress have contributed to depressive symptoms and sociocultural adjustment among international students in the United States. However, hope and optimism were found to have a moderating effect on these depressive symptoms, even though these variables do not have a significant direct effect on psychological adjustment [78]. Self-efficacy, and strong social support from other people, friends or university [79] are other important strategies that help international students to increase their well-being and overcome psychological problems; so too are religious factors such as faith, identity, values and beliefs [80, 81].

The Whole Is Greater Than the Sum of Its Parts

It is important to understand the nature of relationships between these three domains: academic, sociocultural, and psychological adjustment. Earlier work (e.g., [82, 83]) developed conceptual frameworks which encompass these domains in their attempts to particularise 'the international student experience' across national populations, and to distinguish it from the predominant fields of enquiry related to transnational sojourns by business people, or the experiences of permanent or long-term migrants. The research we present here makes an incremental contribution this literature, by improving understandings of a particular group (Malaysian students) to a particular context (Australian higher education), which may hold some relevance and generalisability to other groups.

Previous studies of international student adjustment show that academic and sociocultural events during adjustment affect students' emotional and well-being [23, 84, 36, 85]. For academic adjustment, the difference in teaching and learning methods between home country and host country [86], a kind of 'academic cultural distance', is associated with other academic difficulties [87]. In addition, academic workload and requirements have exposed international students to stress and psychological problems such as obsessive = compulsive disorder, in the quest to perform well in their study [75].)

In sociocultural and psychological interactive effects, the size of cultural distance between home country and host country contributes to psychological problems [88]. One study, for example, found that the international students who perceive their culture to be lower status than the host country culture tend to have psychological problems such as depression and low self-esteem [54]. English language problems also frequently hinder students from experiencing good communication and interaction with other people in the new environment, thus providing another stressor in the psychological domain [89]. International students also have a tendency to experience loneliness due to the absence of their original culture, such as food and lifestyle, in the host country [71]. In the early adjustment period, loss of friends and social support in their sociocultural sphere, also has impact on international students' initial academic and psychological adjustment [90].

Considering these two types of interactive relationships across the domains, it is important to understand how international students feel and experience academic and sociocultural issues and problems. We argue that the interactions of academic, sociocultural, and psychological domains determine the overall adjustment of international students; and because of interactive effects, it is not enough to consider one domain by itself. In the following section, we outline a study exploring all three domains among one international student cohort.

TAKING AN INTEGRATED APPROACH

In this section, we outline a study exploring Malaysian International University Students' (MIUSs') adjustment experiences in Australia. As an exploratory study using a mixed methodologies approach – qualitative and quantitative – this research study was designed to capture the voices of MIUSs in relation to various aspects, academic, sociocultural and psychological, of adjustment.

To address a large research gap surrounding MIUSs, an exploratory sequential mixed methods design (ESMMD) recommended by [91] was adopted, to: firstly, qualitatively explore MIUS adjustment experience, using a small sample size in selected states in Australia; and secondly, determine whether the qualitative results of MIUSs adjustment experience could be quantitatively generalised to a large MIUS population. In conjunction with both sets of findings, this method allows the development and validation of an empirical model for MIUSs' adjustment experiences in Australia.

The research was divided into two phases: Phase 1 used semi-structured interviews and reflective journal entries of MIUSs in New South Wales to provide in-depth illustrations of the experience of students in detailed case studies; and Phase 2 used an online questionnaire survey for MIUSs in several states in Australia to add greater breadth and generalisability to the study.

Gable considered that the integration of case study and survey is an interpretative and positive approach [92]. In the present study, the case study and survey methods were integrated to explore the underpinning issues of MIUS adjustment in Australia. Importantly the study design also allowed for an integrated perspective on the three domains of adjustment.

Data collected in two phases are explained below:

In Phase 1, a purposive sampling technique was used to recruit the participants. A semi-structured interview and reflective journal were conducted with a small sample of MIUSs as case studies (n = 15) across three universities in New South Wales. The data were analysed using a multiple case study and thematic analysis.

In Phase 2, a random sampling technique was used to recruit the participants to represent the population of MIUSs in Australia. The International Students Adjustment Scale (ISAS) online questionnaire developed from the findings of Phase 1 was administered to the new, larger sample of MIUSs (n = 371) in several states in Australia. The data were analysed using a correlation and regression analysis, as it fitted the aim of this study to examine the relationship between the variables and their adjustment domains.

ISAS

As part of the Exploratory Sequential Mixed Methods Design (ESMMD), it is important to highlight the development of the measurable instrument. This section presents a discussion of the International Student Adjustment Scale (ISAS) – the new questionnaire developed as part of the present research, based on Phase 1 qualitative approach-multiple case study findings. There were five stages of development for the ISAS: definition and operationalisation of variables; item development (including review of existing adjustment scale); selection of items and scale; questionnaire reviewing process; and questionnaire design. In the study, a questionnaire was developed to measure MIUSs' adjustment experience in Australia based on all three domains: academic, sociocultural, and psychological adjustment. Building on the qualitative findings, the development of this questionnaire is a technical strategy to operationalise the themes identified in Phase 1. Specifically, this questionnaire operationalises MIUS behaviour, feelings, and thoughts on their adjustment experience quantitatively to measure and evaluate MIUS adjustment across the domains. As such the ISAS is a new holistic measurement of adjustment that specifically represents MIUSs in Australia as international students, but which may be applied to other international student groups in future.

The ISAS was developed with three scales, 16 subscales and 60 items. In this study, an Exploratory Factor Analysis demonstrated the existence of the hypothesised subscales in academic adjustment, sociocultural adjustment, and psychological adjustment with high reliability score (relative to SACQ [93]) that has the highest reported reliability of around 0.70, the overall reliability of ISAS is very high at 0.89).

ADJUSTMENT IS INTERLINKED ACROSS DOMAINS

Both phases of the study illustrated the interconnectedness and interlinking of adjustment issues across the academic, sociocultural, and psychological domains.

Insights from Case Studies

Overall, each of MIUS case study students perceived their personal adjustment experiences in Australia as subject to various life events in academic and social settings. Some of MIUSs perceived their adjustment experiences as a positive and constructive adjustment by reflecting their positive personal transition process in all three adjustment domains. On the other hand, some of MIUSs also perceived their adjustment experience as a negative and destructive adjustment due to various difficulties in one, or two, or all three adjustment domains.

The participants' enrolment as international undergraduate students at Australian universities exposed them to cross-cultural contact in academic life. Malaysian students reported substantial 'academic cultural distance', comparing their current "degree life" in the host country as "difficult and opposite" to their previous study experiences in their home country:

> Assignments and quizzes, not to mention exercises and reading materials, are piling up and suffocating me! They say uni [university] life is relaxing, [but] I find it opposite. (Lim Chin)
> I find it very difficult to adjust to the teaching method [in Australia] compared to the normal direct teaching method back in Malaysia (Eddy)
> The way of teaching in Australia is different from Malaysia. I [am] afraid I cannot absorb the things that the lecturers want to deliver. (Hoi Ling

The differences between previous study experiences in the home country and host country produce various issues related to academic adjustment. For example, some participants reported that they enrolled to start study at the second year of the program. This situation also created academic adjustment difficulties as it amplified the challenges involved. Overall, there were four important themes voiced by the participants regarding the academic adjustment experience: teaching, learning, classroom interaction, and university service and administration.

> I also find my lecturers are teaching very fast and some [of them] speak too fast. I have to spend a lot of time after lectures to slowly digest what was being taught. (Lim Chin)
>
> At first, it is kind of a culture shock... As I enter the lecture hall, most of the students did not bring any lecture materials at all like me... I bring the notebook. (Nana)
>
> During discussion for my project, a Chinese team-mate argued with the lecturer. I find it a little bit rude as a lecturer knows better than a student. A student should at least listen to what the lecturer wants to say (Ariana)
>
> "There are a lot of group assignments for my course, so I need to learn how to cooperate with others during the workshop and lab classes. So, I think this is a big difficulty for me... Because in the past all the things in the school is an individual task. We seldom do it in the group." (Hoi Ling)

Participants experienced sociocultural adjustment in the host country by interaction and engagement with the people and environment in non-academic settings. This process specifically refers to participant adjustment with the different social life, culture, behaviour, value, and atmosphere that arises from the cross-cultural contact. In this study, there are four components of sociocultural adjustment that emerged from the interviews and reflective journals: friendship, community, activity, and discrimination

Regarding the different sociocultural environment between the home country and host country, the majority of the participants did not experience significant culture shock but two participants reported that they felt "disturbed" by Australian culture.

> Easter just started. Although it is a nice celebration but the young are having all kinds of party and getting drunk which I find really disturbing. (Eddy)
>
> I am trying to absorb the Australian way of life but having so many Malaysian friends is hindering the process. So, I joined Toastmasters to help me making Australian friends and it sort of works. (Shan)
>
> As we expected, the next morning we found a short note from our neighbour who stayed at the second level. They asked our cooperation not to make any loud noise that can disturb their peace. I was so pissed off. As I knew, we should not make any noise during the night but not during the

daylight. The other neighbours were so cool about it but not 'this' neighbour. (Nana)

In this study, psychological adjustment refers to participants' emotional well-being resulting from both the positive and negative events in academic and social settings during the adjustment process, comprising academic and sociocultural aspects. Overall, there are five main issues related to the psychological adjustment experience arising from interviews and reflective journals: stress, depression, homesickness, loneliness, and happiness. Participants' emotions and feelings were affected by their adjustment experience as early as from their arrival in the host country. One participant expressed her "mixed feelings" after arrival in Sydney:

> At 7.30 am, I was safely touched down in Sydney airport. I feel happy, nervous, and scared at the same time. I am happy because of my dream had come true, nervous because this is my first time [arrive] in the foreign country, and scared as I did not know where should I go after this as I feel completely as a stranger here. (Ayda)
>
> I felt that I could not 100% understand what the lecturers were talking about during the class. I afraid this [problem] affect my studies. (Hoi Ling)
>
> Last week we have a test, but our score is really bad... [for] the whole class... so it is kind of give an impact to us ...especially for me... it is very depressing. (Eddy)
>
> I miss my country! The food and the people and also the things I can get from Malaysia. (Lim Chin)

APPLYING THE INTERNATIONAL STUDENT ADJUSTMENT SCALE (ISAS)

In addition to the case studies, we explored the relationship between the domains, academic, sociocultural, and psychological adjustment, in a larger sample survey with 371 MIUS responses on the ISAS online questionnaire. We were interested to ask: what are the measured associations between the three domains, academic, sociocultural, and psychological adjustment?

MIUSs perceived all adjustment domains as having some issues for them over the last three months. A few descriptive results show that 62.3% of MIUSs felt it hard to survive in the host country and 44.5% MIUSs doubted their ability to adapt to the new environment. Encouragingly, some 69.5% of MIUSs reported conquering their fears to develop connections with the people and environment in the host country regardless of the difficulties experienced during adjustment. In the following section, we outline the issues relating to each domain and then examine interrelationships across domains.

The overall mean score for the academic adjustment scale was average, at 3.74 (SD = .37, Min = 2.56, Max = 4.94), indicating that the majority of the participants experienced at least moderate issues of academic adjustment. In specific terms, learning assessment (M = 4.01, SD = .55), learning activities (M = 4.00, SD = .45), and teaching (M = 4.03, SD = .48) had the highest mean score among the subscales, indicating that MIUSs agreed that learning assessment and learning activities were important issues during academic adjustment. On the other hand, classroom interaction (M = 3.33, SD = .66) recorded the lowest mean score, indicating that MIUSs perceived classroom interaction is the milder issue in relation to academic adjustment. Different international cohorts, however, might experience things differently to this Malaysian group of students.

The overall mean score for the sociocultural adjustment scale (SAS) was at M = 3.80 (SD = .35, Min = 2.00, Max = 4.96), indicating that MIUSs on average agreed that they had experienced at least moderate issues of sociocultural adjustment in the new environment. Subscales for 'cultural differences' and 'activities' each recorded a high mean score, at 4.00 (SD = .41) and 3.93 (SD = .44), respectively. Meanwhile, 'discrimination' scored the lowest mean value, at 3.47 (SD = .81). These results indicate that MIUSs agreed that cultural differences and social activities in the new environment were important issues of sociocultural adjustment but discrimination was being a more moderate issue in the last three months.

The overall mean score for the psychological adjustment scale (PAS) was average, at 3.53 (SD = .37, Min = 2.34, Max = 4.78), indicating that MIUSs tend to report positive psychological adjustment in Australia. For the sub-scales, happiness reported the highest mean score, at 4.00 (SD = .49). This indicates that on average MIUSs agreed that they experienced happiness in the last three months during adjustment and the majority did not report experiencing other psychological issues.

The previous mean scores for each domain variable were compared to each other. The results indicate that the sociocultural adjustment (M = 3.99, SD = .33) mean score is slightly higher than academic (M = 3.85, SD = .37) and psychological adjustment (M = 3.58, SD = .48) scores. This means that MIUSs agreed that they had experienced all three types of adjustment while living and studying in Australia over the last three months.

The relationships between all main scales and subscales were investigated using the Pearson product-moment correlation coefficient. Preliminary analyses were performed to ensure no violation of the assumptions of normality, linearity, and homoscedasticity. The results for correlation analysis in Table 1 show that the three adjustment scales, academic, sociocultural, and psychological adjustment, were significantly correlated. The strongest positive correlation was between sociocultural adjustment and psychological adjustment, $r(369) = .62$, $p < .001$. Academic adjustment also positively correlated with psychological adjustment, $r(369) = .47$, $p < .001$. These results mean that academic and sociocultural adjustments have a direct impact on psychological adjustment. MIUSs who had relatively positive academic and sociocultural adjustment experiences tended to have a better psychological adjustment experience in Australia.

The correlation analysis between all subscales shows that learning activities were significantly correlated with friendship, $r(369) = .40$, $p < .01$, community, $r(369) = .43$, $p < .01$, social activities, $r(369) = .44$, $p < .01$, and happiness, $r(369) = .41$, $p < .01$. Communication also positively correlated with discrimination, $r(369) = .44$, $p < .01$ and stress, $r(369) = .42$, $p < .01$ Teaching subscales positively correlates with happiness, $r(369) = .40$, $p < .01$. In sociocultural adjustment, activities were significantly positively correlated with happiness, $r(369) = .41$, $p < .01$, and discrimination subscale was positively correlated with stress, $r(369) = .59$, $p < .01$ and loneliness, $r(369) = .48$, $p < .01$. On the other hand, homesickness had a weak, positive correlation with most of the subscales.

Conclusion

Existing literature on adjustment over the last seven decades [69] has examined and discussed adjustment issues among different international student populations around the world. We put forward a holistic approach and suggest that fragmented approaches, examining only academic adjustment aspects for example, provide an unsatisfactory picture of the issues involved.

This study is also a significant driver towards understanding MIUS adjustment, which has rarely been examined. We find MIUSs in Australia report some unique patterns of adjustment issues or problems. Our findings contrast with the limited previous studies of Malaysian students' adjustment; and highlight how consideration of local lifestyle can help in sociocultural adjustment as well as documenting high levels of happiness in psychological adjustment. The different story created by MIUSs in Australia reinforces the existing literature of MIUSs adjustment issues and illustrates the need for integrated approaches that can account for the complexity of interactions between the students and their host environments.

By viewing MIUSs adjustment experience holistically, our study findings suggest that the ups and downs in each adjustment domain are the result of complex interaction between developmental domains and are not fixed to any adjustment patterns. With reference to the three adjustment styles [80], MIUSs adjustment in Australia generally can be classified as a positive and connected. The majority of MIUSs experience a lower level of stress and have a strong connection with the new environment. MIUSs also are able to adjust to the new environment, and deal with the adjustment problems or issues, using various strategies, and do not suffer from any extreme psychological condition during adjustment.

These findings show the interactions or relationships between the academic, sociocultural, and psychological adjustment domains, and how self-initiative and social support strategies can be repeatedly used to overcome MIUSs' adjustment issues or problems adapting within the new environment. The empirical results of the relationships between all adjustment domains strongly support the mutual interaction of academic, sociocultural, and psychological adjustment domains.

Integrating findings in Phase 1 and 2, it can be concluded that both academic and sociocultural adjustment have moderate effect on psychological adjustment. Sociocultural adjustment appears as the strongest predictor of the psychological adjustment. This finding indicates that MIUSs who are actively participate in social activities and have a strong relationship with the Malaysian community, tended to have a better psychological well-being and vice versa. In Phase 1, both factors report as strong contributors to the emotional well-being, but results in Phase 2 indicate that academic factor have a more minor direct contribution to MIUSs' psychological well-being. However, in phase 2, it was clear that academic adjustment is the most central element in MIUS adjustment. Thus, academic adjustment impacts strongly upon social adjustment and also directly and indirectly (via social adjustment) upon psychological adjustment.

These findings have important implications for supporting MIUS cohorts and also other international students. They reinforce the understanding that the quality of academic experience is highly influential, perhaps the defining element, in the student adjustment experience. Institutional efforts to improve academic adjustment need to be built around understanding of cultural distance and other factors specific to international cohorts; and also understanding of the social and psychological adjustment issues. It is not enough, for example, to provide innovation in teaching and learning without considering how that might be received by the diverse range international students. However, there is great promise for institutions to act proactively, engaging international students not only in classes, but in social realms, so that there are many opportunities for communication and shared learning. Our study's findings suggest that thoughtful investment in programs related to academic and social adjustment, can have positive knock-on effects on psychological adjustment. They can provide multiple positive outcomes, on learning as well as overall happiness, and are indeed preferable and likely more cost-effective than remedial student mental health services. Understanding these dynamics, and the importance of sensitivity to the diversity of experience seen across individuals and cohorts, is central to the sustainability and prosperity of the international education sector.

REFERENCES

[1] Verbik, Line, and Veronica Lasanowski. "International student mobility: Patterns and trends." *World Education News and Reviews* 20, no. 10 (2007): 1-16.

[2] Neubauer, Deane E., and John N. Hawkins. "Prospects for Higher Education in the Midst of Globalization." In *The Palgrave Handbook of Asia Pacific Higher Education*, pp. 57-72. Palgrave Macmillan, New York, 2016.

[3] King, Russell, and Parvati Raghuram. "International student migration: Mapping the field and new research agendas." *Population, Space and Place* 19, no. 2 (2013): 127-137.

[4] Organization for Economic Co-operation and Development OECD. "*Education at a Glance 2018: OECD Indicators.*" OECD Publishing, Paris. (2018). http://dx.doi.org/10.1787/eag-2018-en.

[5] Organization for Economic Co-operation and Development OECD. "*Education at a Glance 2016: OECD Indicators.*" OECD Publishing, Paris. (2019).

[6] Findlay, Allan M., Russell King, Fiona M. Smith, Alistair Geddes, and Ronald Skeldon. "World class? An investigation of globalisation, difference and international student mobility." *Transactions of the Institute of British Geographers* 37, no. 1 (2012): 118-131.

[7] Wilkins, Stephen, and Jeroen Huisman. "International student destination choice: The influence of home campus experience on the decision to consider branch campuses." *Journal of Marketing for Higher Education* 21, no. 1 (2011): 61-83.

[8] Chen, Liang-Hsuan. "Internationalization or international marketing? Two frameworks for understanding international students' choice of Canadian universities." *Journal of Marketing for Higher Education* 18, no. 1 (2008): 1-33.

[9] Department of Education &Training. "*Research Snapshot November 2016.*" (2016). https://internationaleducation.gov.au/research/Research-Snapshots/Documents/Export%20Income%20FY2015-16.pdf

[10] Arsenault, Patrick. "Internationalization of Higher Education in Turmoil." *The Vermont Connection* 39, no. 1 (2018): 8.

[11] The Times Higher Education and Higher Education Network. "*World universities rankings.*" (2017). https://www.timeshighereducation.com/world-university-rankings.

[12] International Education Research Network. "*Key Trends in International Education Research 2011–14: What Does the Data Tell Us*" (2017). https://www.ieaa.org.au/international-education-research-network/key-trends-2.

[13] Mclachlan, Debra A., and Jessica Justice. "A grounded theory of international student well-being." *Journal of Theory Construction & Testing* 13, no. 1 (2009).

[14] Brown, Lorraine, and Immy Holloway. "The adjustment journey of international postgraduate students at an English university: An ethnographic study." *Journal of Research in International Education* 7, no. 2 (2008): 232-249.

[15] Sherry, Mark, Peter Thomas, and Wing Hong Chui. "International students: A vulnerable student population." *Higher education* 60, no. 1 (2010): 33-46.

[16] Pyvis, David, and Anne Chapman. "Culture shock and the international student 'offshore'." *Journal of research in international education* 4, no. 1 (2005): 23-42.

[17] Yu, Baohua, Peter Bodycott, and Anita S. Mak. "Language and Interpersonal Resource Predictors of Psychological and Sociocultural Adaptation: International Students in Hong Kong." *Journal of Studies in International Education* (2019): 1028315318825336.

[18] Gallucci, Sonia. "International Students: A Minority Group at Risk in Need of Psychological Support." *Journal of Psychological Therapies* 1, no. 2 (2016): 11-16.

[19] Altbach, Philip G. "Impact and adjustment: Foreign students in comparative perspective." *Higher Education* 21, no. 3 (1991): 305-323.

[20] Shankland, Rebecca, Christophe Genolini, Lionel Riou França, Julien-Daniel Guelfi, and Serban Ionescu. "Student adjustment to higher education: the role of alternative educational pathways in coping with the demands of student life." *Higher Education* 59, no. 3 (2010): 353-366.

[21] Samuelowicz, Katherine. "Learning problems of overseas students: Two sides of a story." *Higher Education Research and Development* 6, no. 2 (1987): 121-133.

[22] Ward, Colleen, and Antony Kennedy. "Locus of control, mood disturbance, and social difficulty during cross-cultural transitions." *International Journal of Intercultural Relations* 16, no. 2 (1992): 175-194.

[23] Zhang, Jing, and Patricia Goodson. "Acculturation and psychosocial adjustment of Chinese international students: Examining mediation and moderation effects." *International Journal of Intercultural Relations* 35, no. 5 (2011): 614-627.

[24] Gerdes, Hilary, and Brent Mallinckrodt. "Emotional, social, and academic adjustment of college students: A longitudinal study of retention." *Journal of Counseling & Development* 72, no. 3 (1994): 281-288.

[25] O'Reilly, Aileen, Dermot Ryan, and Tina Hickey. "The psychological well-being and sociocultural adaptation of short-term international students in Ireland." *Journal of college student development* 51, no. 5 (2010): 584-598.

[26] Ladd, Paula D., and Ralph Ruby Jr. "Learning style and adjustment issues of international students." *Journal of education for business* 74, no. 6 (1999): 363-367.

[27] Rienties, Bart, Simon Beausaert, Therese Grohnert, Susan Niemantsverdriet, and Piet Kommers. "Understanding academic performance of international students: the role of ethnicity, academic and social integration." *Higher education* 63, no. 6 (2012): 685-700.

[28] Jackson, Michelle, Sukanya Ray, and Danica Bybell. "International students in the US: Social and psychological adjustment." *Journal of International Students* 3, no. 1 (2013): 17-28.
[29] Department of Education and Training. "International student survey 2014: An overview report." (2015). https://internationaleducation.gov.au/research/research-papers/Documents/ISS%202014%20Report%20Final.pdf.
[30] Department of Education and Training. "2016 International student survey results: Higher education." (2017). https://internationaleducation.gov.au/research/research-papers/Documents/ED17-0018%20International%20Student%20Survey%20HIGHER%20EDUCATION%20Infographic_05.pdf.
[31] Ryan, Roberta, Ben Dowler, Sophi Bruce, Sasindu Gamage, and Alan Morris. "*The wellbeing of international students in the city of Sydney.*" (2016).
[32] Rajapaksa, Sushama, and Lauren Dundes. "It's a long way home: International student adjustment to living in the United States." *Journal of College Student Retention: Research, Theory & Practice* 4, no. 1 (2002): 15-28.
[33] Kagan, Henya, and Jo Cohen. "Cultural adjustment of international students." *Psychological Science* 1, no. 2 (1990): 133-137.
[34] Fritz, Marie Väfors, Dorothy Chin, and Valerie DeMarinis. "Stressors, anxiety, acculturation and adjustment among international and North American students." *International Journal of Intercultural Relations* 32, no. 3 (2008): 244-259.
[35] Yakobov, Esther, Tomas Jurcik, Liza Solopieieva-Jurcikova, and Andrew G. Ryder. "Acculturation and expectations: Unpacking adjustment mechanisms within the Russian-speaking community in Montreal." *International Journal of Intercultural Relations* 68 (2019): 67-76.
[36] Zhou, Yuefang, Divya Jindal-Snape, Keith Topping, and John Todman. "Theoretical models of culture shock and adaptation in international students in higher education." *Studies in higher education* 33, no. 1 (2008): 63-75.

[37] Burns, Robert B. "Study and stress among first year overseas students in an Australian university." *Higher Education Research and Development* 10, no. 1 (1991): 61-77.
[38] Hellstén, Meeri. "Students in transition: Needs and experiences of international students in Australia." (2002).
[39] Rienties, Bart, Simon Beausaert, Therese Grohnert, Susan Niemantsverdriet, and Piet Kommers. "Understanding academic performance of international students: the role of ethnicity, academic and social integration." *Higher education* 63, no. 6 (2012): 685-700.
[40] Andrade, Maureen Snow. "International students in English-speaking universities: Adjustment factors." *Journal of Research in International education* 5, no. 2 (2006): 131-154.
[41] Kambouropoulos, Alexa. "An examination of the adjustment journey of international students studying in Australia." *The Australian Educational Researcher* 41, no. 3 (2014): 349-363.
[42] Miquelon, Paule, Robert J. Vallerand, Frédérick ME Grouzet, and Geneviève Cardinal. "Perfectionism, academic motivation, and psychological adjustment: An integrative model." *Personality and Social Psychology Bulletin* 31, no. 7 (2005): 913-924.
[43] Yusoff, Yusliza Mohd. "Self-efficacy, perceived social support, and psychological adjustment in international undergraduate students in a public higher education institution in Malaysia." *Journal of Studies in International Education* 16, no. 4 (2012): 353-371.
[44] Ramburuth, Prem, and John McCormick. "Learning diversity in higher education: A comparative study of Asian international and Australian students." *Higher education* 42, no. 3 (2001): 333-350.
[45] Kennett, Deborah J., Maureen J. Reed, and Amanda S. Stuart. "The impact of reasons for attending university on academic resourcefulness and adjustment." *Active Learning in Higher Education* 14, no. 2 (2013): 123-133.
[46] Bianchi, Constanza. "Satisfiers and dissatisfiers for international students of higher education: An exploratory study in Australia." *Journal of Higher Education Policy and Management* 35, no. 4 (2013): 396-409.

[47] Yusuf, Muhammed. "Investigating relationship between self-efficacy, achievement motivation, and self-regulated learning strategies of undergraduate students: A study of integrated motivational models." *Procedia-Social and Behavioral Sciences* 15 (2011): 2614-2617.

[48] Khawaja, Nigar G., and Helen M. Stallman. "Understanding the coping strategies of international students: A qualitative approach." *Journal of Psychologists and Counsellors in Schools* 21, no. 2 (2011): 203-224.

[49] Li, Gang, Wei Chen, and Jing-Lin Duanmu. "Determinants of international students' academic performance: A comparison between Chinese and other international students." *Journal of Studies in International Education* 14, no. 4 (2010): 389-405.

[50] Ramsay, Sheryl, Michelle Barker, and Elizabeth Jones. "Academic Adjustment and Learning Processes: a comparison of international and local students in first-year university." *Higher Education Research & Development* 18, no. 1 (1999): 129-144.

[51] Zhang, Yanyin, and Yinan Mi. "Another look at the language difficulties of international students." *Journal of Studies in international Education* 14, no. 4 (2010): 371-388.

[52] Pan, Jia-Yan, and Daniel Fu Keung Wong. "Acculturative stressors and acculturative strategies as predictors of negative affect among Chinese international students in Australia and Hong Kong: A cross-cultural comparative study." *Academic Psychiatry* 35, no. 6 (2011): 376-381.

[53] Hofstede, Geert. "Cultural dimensions in management and planning." *Asia Pacific journal of management* 1, no. 2 (1984): 81-99.

[54] Furukawa, Toshiaki. "Cultural distance and its relationship to psychological adjustment of international exchange students." *Psychiatry and clinical neurosciences* 51, no. 3 (1997): 87-91.

[55] Asmar, Christine. "Politicising student difference: The Muslim experience." In *International Relations*, pp. 129-157. Emerald Group Publishing Limited, 2005.

[56] Novera, Isvet Amri. "Indonesian postgraduate students studying in Australia: An examination of their academic, social and cultural

experiences." *International Education Journal* 5, no. 4 (2004): 475-487.

[57] Swami, Viren. "Predictors of sociocultural adjustment among sojourning Malaysian students in Britain." *International Journal of Psychology* 44, no. 4 (2009): 266-273.

[58] Kim, Hye Yeong. "International graduate students' difficulties: Graduate classes as a community of practices." *Teaching in Higher Education* 16, no. 3 (2011): 281-292.

[59] Coles, Rebecca, and Viren Swami. "The sociocultural adjustment trajectory of international university students and the role of university structures: A qualitative investigation." *Journal of Research in International Education* 11, no. 1 (2012): 87-100.

[60] Bista, Krishna. "Asian international students' college experience: Relationship between quality of personal contact and gains in learning." *Journal of International and Global Studies Volume* 6, no. 2 (2015): 39.

[61] Asmar, Christine. "Internationalising students: reassessing diasporic and local student difference." *Studies in Higher Education* 30, no. 3 (2005): 291-309.

[62] Ward, Colleen, and Wendy Searle. "The impact of value discrepancies and cultural identity on psychological and sociocultural adjustment of sojourners." *International Journal of Intercultural Relations* 15, no. 2 (1991): 209-224.

[63] Wang, Chia-Chih DC, and Brent Mallinckrodt. "Acculturation, attachment, and psychosocial adjustment of Chinese/Taiwanese international students." *Journal of Counseling Psychology* 53, no. 4 (2006): 422.

[64] Terry, Deborah J., Rebecca N. Pelly, Richard N. Lalonde, and Joanne R. Smith. "Predictors of cultural adjustment: Intergroup status relations and boundary permeability." *Group Processes & Intergroup Relations* 9, no. 2 (2006): 249-264.

[65] Li, Andrew, and Michael B. Gasser. "Predicting Asian international students' sociocultural adjustment: A test of two mediation models."

International Journal of Intercultural Relations 29, no. 5 (2005): 561-576.

[66] Kağnıcı, Dilek Yelda. "The role of multicultural personality in predicting university adjustment of international students in Turkey." *International Journal for the Advancement of Counselling* 34, no. 2 (2012): 174-184.

[67] Yan, Kun, and David C. Berliner. "Chinese international students' personal and sociocultural stressors in the United States." *Journal of college student development* 54, no. 1 (2013): 62-84.

[68] Akanwa, Emmanuel E. "International students in western developed countries: History, challenges, and prospects." *Journal of International Students* 5, no. 3 (2015): 271-284.

[69] Lysgaard, Sverre. "Adjustment in a foreign society: Norwegian Fulbright grantees visiting the United States. International Social Science Bulletin, 7, 45-51." *Journal of Counseling Psychology* 53, no. 1 (1955): 126-131.

[70] Brown, Lorraine, and Immy Holloway. "The initial stage of the international sojourn: excitement or culture shock?." *British Journal of Guidance & Counselling* 36, no. 1 (2008): 33-49.

[71] Sawir, Erlenawati, Simon Marginson, Ana Deumert, Chris Nyland, and Gaby Ramia. "Loneliness and international students: An Australian study." *Journal of studies in international education* 12, no. 2 (2008): 148-180.

[72] Sawir, Erlenawati, Simon Marginson, Ana Deumert, Chris Nyland, and Gaby Ramia. "Loneliness and international students: An Australian study." *Journal of studies in international education* 12, no. 2 (2008): 148-180.

[73] Tananuraksakul, Noparat, and David Hall. "International students' emotional security and dignity in an Australian context: An aspect of psychological well-being." *Journal of Research in International Education* 10, no. 2 (2011): 189-200.

[74] Pedersen, Eric R., Clayton Neighbors, Mary E. Larimer, and Christine M. Lee. "Measuring sojourner adjustment among American students

studying abroad." *International Journal of Intercultural Relations* 35, no. 6 (2011): 881-889.

[75] Khawaja, Nigar Gohar, and Jenny Dempsey. "Psychological distress in international university students: An Australian study." *Journal of Psychologists and Counsellors in Schools* 17, no. 1 (2007): 13-27.

[76] Mori, Sakurako Chako. "Addressing the mental health concerns of international students." *Journal of counseling & development* 78, no. 2 (2000): 137-144.

[77] Yakunina, Elena S., Ingrid K. Weigold, Arne Weigold, Sanja Hercegovac, and Noha Elsayed. "The multicultural personality: Does it predict international students' openness to diversity and adjustment?." *International Journal of Intercultural Relations* 36, no. 4 (2012): 533-540.

[78] Esch, Laura, and Valerie A. Ubbes. "A Culturally Appropriate Framework for Educating Collegiate International Students about Alcohol." *International Electronic Journal of Health Education* 12 (2009): 244-252.

[79] Baker, Gail, and Ken Hawkins. "The international student journey." *Australian Universities' Review, The* 48, no. 2 (2006): 20.

[80] Russell, Jean, Garry Thomson, and Doreen Rosenthal. "International student use of university health and counselling services." *Higher Education* 56, no. 1 (2008): 59-75.

[81] Abdullah, Siti Salina Binti. "Help seeking behavior among Malaysian international students in Australia." *International Journal of Business and Social Science* 2, no. 23 (2011).

[82] Schartner, Alina, and Tony Johnstone Young. "Towards an integrated conceptual model of international student adjustment and adaptation." *European Journal of Higher Education* 6, no. 4 (2016): 372-386.

[83] Young, Tony J., Peter G. Sercombe, Itesh Sachdev, Rola Naeb, and Alina Schartner. "Success factors for international postgraduate students' adjustment: exploring the roles of intercultural competence, language proficiency, social contact and social support." *European Journal of Higher Education* 3, no. 2 (2013): 151-171.

[84] Zhang, Jing, and Patricia Goodson. "Predictors of international students' psychosocial adjustment to life in the United States: A systematic review." *International journal of intercultural relations* 35, no. 2 (2011): 139-162.

[85] Sam, David Lackland. "Satisfaction with life among international students: An exploratory study." *Social indicators research* 53, no. 3 (2001): 315-337.

[86] Smith, Rachel A., and Nigar G. Khawaja. "A review of the acculturation experiences of international students." *International Journal of intercultural relations* 35, no. 6 (2011): 699-713.

[87] Townsend, Barbara K. "*University Practices That Hinder the Academic Success of Community College Transfer Students.*" (1993).

[88] Shupe, Ellen I. "Clashing cultures: A model of international student conflict." *Journal of Cross-Cultural Psychology* 38, no. 6 (2007): 750-771.

[89] Yeh, Christine J., and Mayuko Inose. "International students' reported English fluency, social support satisfaction, and social connectedness as predictors of acculturative stress." *Counselling Psychology Quarterly* 16, no. 1 (2003): 15-28.

[90] Hayes, Richard L., and Heng-Rue Lin. "Coming to America: Developing social support systems for international students." *Journal of Multicultural counseling and Development* 22, no. 1 (1994): 7-16.

[91] Creswell, John W., and J. David Creswell. *Research design: Qualitative, quantitative, and mixed methods approaches.* Sage publications, 2017.

[92] Gable, Guy G. "Integrating case study and survey research methods: an example in information systems." *European journal of information systems* 3, no. 2 (1994): 112-126.

[93] Baker, Robert W., and Bohdan Siryk. "Measuring adjustment to college." *Journal of counseling psychology* 31, no. 2 (1984): 179.

In: Exploring the Opportunities ... ISBN: 978-1-53616-241-7
Editor: Michael Allison © 2019 Nova Science Publishers, Inc.

Chapter 3

EMOTIONAL SUPPORTS AND ACADEMIC STRESSES AMONG YOUNG CHINESE INTERNATIONAL STUDENTS

Xi Lin[1],*, Shu Su[2] and Alyssa McElwain[3]
[1]Department of Interdiciplinary Professions,
East Carolina University, Greenville, NC, US
[2]Department of Early Childhood, Youth, and Family Studies,
Ball State University, Muncie, IN, US
[3]Department of Family and Consumer Sciences,
University of Wyoming, Laramie, WY, US

ABSTRACT

Using a multi-university sample, this chapter presents a study of how types of emotional support play a role in young Chinese international students' experience of academic stresses. A total number of 125 young Chinese sojourners who are aged between 18 to 26 participated in the study. Results indicate that a higher level of English proficiency, more

---

* Corresponding Author's Email: linxi18@ecu.edu.

parent involvement, and a lower level of loneliness reduce their academic stresses, while a closer friendship would increase their academic stresses. It is expected that this chapter will help higher education professionals to better understand and support today's young Chinese international students who study in the US. This chapter can further shed light on suggestions for higher education professionals both in the US and other countries to consider strategies to help young international students in their institutions.

Keywords: Chinese international students, academic stresses, language proficiency, social support

INTRODUCTION

International students coming to the US for degree seeking purposes are younger and younger. According to reports from the Institute of International Education (2013, 2014, 2017), before 2013, the number of international students pursuing graduate degrees was greater than that of students seeking bachelor's degrees. However, beginning around 2013 to 2014, the number of undergraduate international students in the US reached 301,144 and it exceeded the number of graduate international students (296,161). Since then, the number of undergraduate international students continued growing and recently reached 362,666 in the year of 2016-2017.

Chinese students comprise 32.5% of the total number of all international students (Institute of International Education, 2017). Among Chinese international students, many of them are 18 years old or younger when they begin their education in the US. Studies note that the pursuit of education among young Chinese has provided a rationale for travelling overseas and it is socially and politically acceptable (King & Gardiner, 2015). Several reasons were identified for the prevalence of this trend (Barclay, Weinandt, & Barclay, 2017). First, many Chinese parents today believe it is beneficial to gain a new cultural view and better language skills. They believe that if their children study abroad at a younger age they may have better career opportunities after completing school. Second, with China's rapid economic growth, members of the Chinese middle class have acquired personal wealth and can afford tuition at universities abroad. Third, the opening of economic policy in China encouraged Westernization of both culture and education, which further increased interest in studying abroad.

While the influx of young Chinese undergraduates to the United States is a positive trend, these young adults may suffer more academic stresses than their peers both in China and the US because they often study and live in the US alone for the first time (Gardiner & Kwek, 2017). Additionally, as non-English speakers, these students may sometimes struggle with school because they need to spend more time and effort in adapting to the new language, different learning and teaching styles, and the various requirements of assignments in US institutions (Liao, & Wei, 2014). Previous studies noted that academic stresses are salient acculturative stresses for many Chinese international students (Smith & Khawaja, 2011; Wan, 2001). Meanwhile, social support could help in reducing the academic stresses among these students and to assist them to transit to a new culture smoothly (Alharbi & Smith, 2018). Therefore, in order to better help the rising young Chinese international students, this study aims to investigate factors that would help in managing their academic stresses.

LITERATURE REVIEW

Previous studies conclude that the influx of international students has positive impacts on the US, culturally and economically (Forbush & Foncault-Welles, 2016). The unique cultural heritage these students bring with them could diversify the population, and increase the awareness and appreciation of other cultures (Bevis, 2002). Additionally, international students also add intellectual capital to the country and workforce, as well as positively influence the country's financial capital (Forbush & Foncault-Welles, 2016; Smith & Khawaja, 2011). Many of these students go on to contribute to the best and brightest scientific minds in the US (Hawthorne, 2010; Zucker & Darby, 2007). Therefore, as international students provide various benefits to the US, their academic success, physical and psychological wellbeing are significant issues that warrant attention

(Chirkov, Vansteenkiste, Tao, & Lynch, 2007). Several factors have been reported as the predictors of these students' stress such as English language proficiency, age upon arrival, length of stay, educational level, and socio-economic status (Constantine, Okazaki, & Utsey, 2004; Kuo & Roysircar, 2004).

Insufficient English Proficiency

Previous studies reported that international students usually lack English proficiency (Constanitine et al., 2004; Brauss, Lin & Baker, 2015). Hwang and Ting (2008) noted that although students from Asian countries often have high English test score from Educational Testing Services (ETS), they still face great language barriers in daily communication. Meanwhile, language ability is noted as negatively correlated with students' academic stresses (Kuo & Roysircar, 2004). Specifically, international students with a lower level of English proficiency typically have more difficulties in understanding course content and participating in classroom discussion. Additionally, language barriers also prevent them from communicating with their American peers, faculty, and members of the community (Bai, 2016). Chen and Ross (2015) furthermore reported that the greatest adjustment issue among Chinese international undergraduate students is their inadequate English proficiency, and this challenge would then lead to higher level of academic stresses.

Loneliness

Several factors may predispose young Chinese international students to loneliness. A low level of English language proficiency may lead to students' loneliness (Alharbi & Smith, 2018). Cultural distance could also lead to loneliness. For example, Barron and colleagues (2007) indicated that many Chinese international students reported loneliness and homesickness as a concern during their first semester when studying abroad. Similarly,

Sawir and colleagues (2008) interviewed 200 international students and discovered that 65% of them experienced loneliness, especially in the months immediately following their arrival in the host country. Loneliness has been identified to be negatively associated with academic success, and international students who often feel depressed due to loneliness tend not to focus on their studies (Banjong, 2015).

Lack of Family and Friend Support

Loneliness is more likely to occur when one is far away from family and friends, particularly when there is a loss of contact with families and general loss of previous social networks (Alharbi & Smith, 2018). Furthermore, such loss of contact is identified as a major type of loneliness among international students. Social support, which refers to the provision of psychological and material resources from others to help the individual experiencing stress (Crockett et al., 2007) has been identified as a significant means for international students to manage their transition to a new culture. Researchers concluded that social support mostly comes from one's family, friends and peer group, work colleagues, members of the community, and significant others (Alharbi & Smith, 2018; Zimet, Dahlem, Zimet, & Farley, 1988).

Studies reveal that social support could facilitate adjustment and academic achievement as well as managing life stress (Liu & Winder, 2014). For example, Murray and colleagues (2013) noted that social support positively contributed to university adjustment among students with disabilities during their transition into university. Additionally, Yusoff and Othman (2011) indicated that psychological adjustment was highly correlated with perceived social support from family, friends, and a significant other for international students. Similarly, support from family members and close friends are reported as a means to reduce international students' academic success (Neri & Ville, 2008). Cai (2016) also implied that international students who receive more social support tend to experience lower levels of stress, and their academic motivation is enhanced by receiving support from their family and friends (Chen, Wiium, Dimitrova, & Chen, 2017).

Of all the international students, Chinese students form the largest group in the US institutions (Institute of International Education, 2017). Researchers noted that Chinese students are usually the least adjusted group among all international students, and they often have high levels of stress (Galchenko & van de Vijver, 2007; Hazen & Alberts, 2006). They usually struggle with performing well in the American classroom, adapting to the new cultural customs and norms, and establishing meaningful relationships with local peers and instructors (Hazen & Alberts, 2006; Yan & Berliner, 2013). However, among many previous studies, most of them investigate international students as a whole group without specific attention to subpopulations. As the population of young Chinese international undergraduate students is growing rapidly, it is important to investigate the relationship between academic stresses, the adjustment issues, and the support these young sojourners receive. It is expected that this study would help educational professionals to better understand those young travelers and better assist them during their journey of seeking degrees in the US.

METHODS

Participants

The target population of this study is undergraduate Chinese students enrolled in universities in the United States. A total number of 138 undergraduate students participated from two universities in this study with 125 usable respondents (usable response rate equals to 91%). Most participants were aged between 18 to 20 (63.2%), some were aged between 21 to 23 (25.6%) and 10.4% of them identified their ages between 24 to 26 years old. Among them, 4.8% did not identify their gender, while the majority of participants were male students (63.2%), with 32% female students. Additionally, most participants reported enrollment in undergraduate or university accelerator programs (77.6%), 19.2% of the participants were freshman, 2.4% were sophomore, 0.8% identified themselves as junior. An accelerator program aims to train ESL international students with intensive academic English skills and/or American culture before beginning regular academic courses. In addition to taking language classes, students in these programs also take some, usually one or two regular academic courses each semester in their chosen majors. Finally, the majority of the participants have resided in the US for less than 1 year (84%).

Instruments

Perception of Academic Stresses Scale (PAS)

The PAS was developed by Bedewy and Gabriel (2015). It is an instrument with 18-item 5-point Likert-type scale, ranging from 1 (*strongly disagree*) to 5 (*strongly agree*). These items evaluate four academic aspects: pressures to perform, perceptions of workload and examinations, self-perceptions, and time restraints. *Pressure to perform* consists of 5 items and assesses excessive stress from competitive peer pressures, parents' expectations, and teachers' critical comments on students' performance. *Perceptions of workload and examinations* consists of 4 items that measure stressors related to excessive workload, lengthy assignments, and worry about failing exams. *Self-perceptions* consists of 5 items and captures academic self-confidence and confidence for success as a student and in their future career as well as confidence in making good academic decisions. *Time Restraints* is assessed by 6 items and refers to stressors as a result of limited time allocated to classes, inability to complete homework, difficulty catching up if behind, and limited time to relax. In each subscale of the PAS, higher scores indicate a higher level of stress. However, a higher score of self-perceptions scale indicates a higher level of confidence in academic success. Five items were reversed-scored. This inventory has an original Cronbach's alpha ranging from 0.60 to 0.63, and the Cronbach's alpha of the instrument in this study ranges from 0.70, 0.62, 0.50, and 0.64, respectively.

Emotional Well-Being

Loneliness was measured using an 8-item 4-point scale (Russell, 1996) from 1 (*never*) to 4 (*always*). The higher score of a scale refers to a higher level of loneliness. Sample items include: "*There is no one I can turn to*," "*I lack companionship*." The Cronbach's alpha of loneliness scale of this study was 0.72.

Language Competency

Students' *English competency* was assessed using a 6-item 5-point Likert-scale ranging from 1 (*strongly disagree*) to 5 (*strongly agree*). Three items were reversed-scored. A higher score indicates a higher level of English competency. Sample items include: "*My English ability prevents me from developing friendships*," "*Others don't understand me when I speak English*." The Cronbach's alpha of this scale in this study was 0.85.

Parenting Strategies

Parenting was assessed using measures of *parental involvement* and *parental support*. Parental involvement refers to how parents oversee and regulate their children's behavior and activities. This scale was measured to by emerging adults' responses to 6 items from the Child Development Project (CDP, Yu et al., 2010). Example questions including "*How often does your parent talk with you about ordinary a daily event in your life*," "*How often does your parent know about your activities at work/school*." It is a 5-point Likert-type scale ranging from 1 (*never*) to 5 (*very frequently*). A higher score of each scale indicates a closer relationship young adult have with their parents. Parental support is indicated by the degree to which young adults turn to their parents for guidance, advice, mentoring, and practical needs (Desjardins & Leadbeater, 2017). This scale was indexed by emerging adults' responses to 3 items (Yu et al., 2010) such as "*How much does your parent provide for your emotional needs*." It is also a 5-point Likert scale rated from 1 (*never*) to 5 (*a lot of time*). A higher score indicates young adults have a higher needs of parent support. The Cronbach's alpha for parental involvement and parent support in this study was 0.70 and 0.60, respectively.

Peer Influences

Best friend relationship and *peer group relationship* (Lansford et al., 2003) were examined. Best friend relationship is a 5-item 5-point Likert-scale ranging from 1 (*strongly disagree*) to 5 (*strongly agree*). Three items were reversed-scored. A higher score indicates a closer friend relationship. Sample items include: "*You and your friend spend a lot of your free time together*," "*If you had personal problems, you can tell your friend about it even if it is something you cannot tell other people.*" Meanwhile, peer group relationship consisted of 4 items with 5-point scale from 1 (*strongly disagree*) to. 5 (*strongly agree*). Similar to best friend relationship, a higher score of the scale refers that the participants more rely on their peer group. Sample items include: "*I spend much time as I can with this group*," "*When my group does something together, others are sure to let me know.*" The Cronbach's alpha for best friend and peer group relationship scale of this study was 0.62 and 0.89, respectively.

Procedure

Researchers conducted an online survey at two universities to evaluate students' college experiences after the approval of Institutional Review Board. The questionnaire was translated into Chinese by two researchers who are fluent in both English and Chinese using the translation and back-translation technique to ensure translation accuracy. The survey allowed participants the language choice of English or Chinese. Data collection took place in March and April 2018 at two universities in the US.

Data Analysis

Data were analyzed using SPSS version 23. A series of multiple regressions using stepwise procedure was conducted to examine the relationship between predictors (pressures to perform, perceptions of workload and examinations, self-perceptions, and time restraints) and criterion variables (loneliness, English competency, parental involvement, parental support, best friend relationship, and peer group relationship) for the purpose of finding the best prediction model for each criterion variable. The significant level of Box's M was set as 0.001 (Mertler, & Vannatta, 2002), and the alpha level was set at 0.05.

RESULTS

We conducted a series of multiple regression using stepwise procedure to investigate the research question: Do levels of loneliness, English competency, parental involvement, parental support, best friend relationship, and peer group relationship predict the level of perceived academic stresses?

Table 1. Relationship between academic stresses and the predictors

DV	R^2	F	df	p	Predictors	β	$t_{(103)}$	p
Pressure to perform	.15	5.84	3,103	.001	Loneliness	0.30	2.25	.027
					Peer group	0.28	2.29	.004
					Parent involvement	-0.28	-2.22	.029
Perceptions of workload & examinations	.132	7.65	2,103	.001	Loneliness	0.39	3.15	.002
					Parent support	0.27	2.74	.007
Self-perceptions	.114	6.48	2,103	.002	Peer group	0.19	2.40	.018
					English competence	0.19	2.28	.025
Time restraints	.108	12.35	1,103	.001	Best friend	-0.33	-3.52	.001

Pressure to Perform

Results indicate that the level of students' loneliness, peer group relationship and parental involvement can predict levels of pressure to perform ($F_{(3, 103)} = 5.84, p = .001$). Additionally, 15% of variance in the level of pressure to perform can be accounted for by the linear combination

(R^2 = .15). For every unit the level of loneliness increases, the level of pressure to perform increases by 0.30 units while the level of other factors remains the same (β = 0.30, $t_{(103)}$ = 2.25, p = .027). For every unit the closeness level of peer group relationship increases, the level of MAP increases by 0.28 units while others stay the same (β = 0.28, $t_{(103)}$ = 2.29, p = .004). However, for every unit the level of parental involvement increases, the level of pressure to perform decreases by 0.29 units while others stays the same (β = -0.28, $t_{(103)}$ = -2.22, p = .029).

Results indicate that young Chinese international students' loneliness and peer group relationship positively predict their pressure to perform academically, while parental involvement negatively influences this academic stress. Specifically, the more loneliness young Chinese international students experience, the more pressure they experience to perform well academically. Additionally, the more they rely on their peers or spend time with their peer groups, the higher level of pressure they receive. Young Chinese students' pressure to perform is lessened when they frequently communicate with parents regarding daily events, feelings, or issues they encounter.

Perceptions of Workload and Examinations

Results show that the level of students' loneliness and parental support can predict levels of their perceptions of workload and examinations ($F_{(2, 103)}$ = 7.65, p = .001). Additionally, 13.2% of variance in the level of pressure to performance can be accounted for by the linear combination (R^2 = .132). For every unit the level of loneliness increases, the level of perceptions of workload and examinations increases by 0.39 units while other factors remain the same (β = 0.39, $t_{(103)}$ = 3.15, p = .002). For every unit the level of parent support increases, the level of perceptions of workload and examinations increases by 0.27 units while others remain the same (β = 0.27, $t_{(103)}$ = 2.74, p = .007).

Data implies that the more lonely young Chinese international students feel, the more pressure they experience in terms of completing assignments and/or pass examinations. Interestingly, these young sojourners feel a higher level of pressure regarding school workload if their parents frequently provide advice and support their practical and emotional needs.

Self-Perceptions

Data indicates that the students' peer group relationships and English competence predict the level of their self-perceptions ($F_{(2, 103)}$ = 6.48, p = .002). Additionally, 11.4% of variance in the level of self-perceptions can be accounted for by the linear combination (R^2 = .114). For every unit the closeness level of peer group relationship increases, the level of self-perceptions increases by 0.19 units while other factor remains the same (β = 0.19, $t_{(103)}$ = 2.40, p = .018). For every unit the level of English competence increases, the level of self-perceptions increases by 0.19 units while peer group relationship remains the same (β = 0.19, $t_{(103)}$ = 2.28, p = .025).

Results show that the more they rely on their peers or the more time they spend with their peer groups, the more they think they will be successful in university or future careers. Meanwhile, those with a higher level of English competence often have more confidence for success as students and in their future career, as well as confidence in making good academic decisions.

Time Restraints

In terms of time restraints, results indicate that only the closeness level of students' best friend relationship can predict the level of time restraints ($F_{(1, 103)}$ = 12.35, p = .001). Meanwhile, 10.8% of variance in the level of self-perceptions can be accounted for by the linear combination (R^2 = .108). For every unit the closeness level of best friend relationship increases, the level of time restraints decreases by 0.33 (β = -0.33, $t_{(103)}$ = -3.52, p = .001). Data indicates that young Chinese international students would experience less time in completing their assignments or catching up with school work if they have a closer friendship such as spending longer time to talk or have fun with their best friends.

CONCLUSION

Discussion

According to the results, young Chinese international students' emotional well-being, language proficiency, parental strategies and peer influence impact their academic stresses. Chinese international students' English proficiency would reduce their stress related to academic self-confidence and their confidence for success as students and their future career, as well as confidence in making good academic decisions. This result echoes previous studies that Chinese students' English proficiency contributes to their acculturative stress (Constantine et al., 2004). Specifically, students who have insufficient English proficiency would experience more difficulty in understanding course content and participating in classroom discussion, which may then lead to a higher level of academic pressure.

Findings indicate that young Chinese international students' loneliness positively associates with their stress from competitive peer pressure, parents' expectations, and teachers' critical comments on their performance. They would experience a higher level of peer pressure and to meet the expectations from their parents and instructors. Additionally, the feeling of being lonely also impacts their stress related to excessive workload, lengthy assignments, and their worry about failing exams. These results mirror a previous study that loneliness usually negatively correlates with students' academic success (Banjong, 2015). Students who experience a higher level of loneliness may likely pay less attention to their studies.

Additionally, social support has a significant influence on young Chinese international students' academic stresses. In terms of parenting strategies, parental involvement would reduce their pressure from competitive peer pressure, parents' expectations, and teachers' critical comments on their performance. This finding mirrors previous conclusions that parental involvement usually has positive impacts on student development, and those with highly involved parents usually have greater personal competence which would also enhance their personal and social development (Carney-Hall, 2008; Shoup et al., 2009), and these students would have better life and psychological adjustment (Fingerman et al., 2012).

Interestingly, parental support increases their stress related to excessive workload, lengthy assignments, and their worry about failing exams. This result contrasts with previous studies that parental support would facilitate young adults' adjustment and well-being, as well as influencing their educational and occupational outcomes within the college context (Desjardins & Leadbeater, 2017; Murphy, Blustein, Bohlig, & Platt, 2010; Ratelle et al., 2005). Studies indicate that Asian parents usually have high expectations of academic achievement for their children, thus these students are found to bear a greater fear of academic failure (Bai, 2016; Wei et al., 2007). However, facing a new environment, many Asian students may find it difficult to keep a good performance as before. Therefore, it is possible that the young Chinese students experience a higher level of pressure to meet their family expectations especially when receiving more supports such as financial support from their parents.

In terms of peer influence, findings indicate that those young sojourners usually have a higher level of stress related to academic performance and time to complete school work if they have a closer relationship with friends and their peer group. These findings argue with previous studies that international students who receive more social support tend to experience a lower level of acculturative stress (Bai, 2016). Although studies indicate various social support (e.g., family, friends, significant others) is associated with positive behaviors toward university adjustment and would assist in coping with academic stresses among international students (Chao, 2012; Salami, 2011; Rahat & Iihan, 2016), this study reports that spending more time or always having fun with peers or best friend increases Chinese young sojourners' academic stresses. However, their confidence in academic success was reported as increasing. It is possible that even though they are worried about the time to complete their academic work, they would encourage each other which then enhance their academic confidence. More research is needed to examine this assumption.

Implications

Studying abroad is usually a young Chinese youth's first experience of independent travel and living in another country without their parents and friends. Thus, it is important to help them adjust to the new environment and the new culture. Universities may consider strategies regarding reducing their feelings of loneliness, such as providing programs that connect those Chinese young sojourners with local students in order to establish meaningful relationship and friendship. Furthermore, universities should introduce the school counseling center during orientation and encourage Chinese international students to visit the center if needed. Moreover, it would be helpful for university international student office to conduct surveys or related means to keep track with these young students' emotional well-being every semester in order to provide them timely assistance.

Because parental involvement can reduce young Chinese international students' academic stresses, universities may consider involving parents to help those young sojourners especially during their first semester. For example, schools could send a letter to the parents emphasizing the importance of their involvement and encouragement, as well as the significance of releasing their children's pressure through establishing proper expectations. It is also beneficial for young Chinese international students to establish friendships with their peers or join communities that share similar interests, which may enhance their academic confidence. Meanwhile, it is necessary for universities to inform these young students in terms of balancing their study time and the time they spend with their groups. Finally, it is important to improve young Chinese international students' English proficiency and communication skills in order to better understand the course content and to better adjust to the US academic culture. Therefore, instructors should motivate these students to seek help from academic support such as study partner or tutor and campus writing centers. Moreover, based on the English test score (e.g., Test of English as a Foreign Language [TOEFL]), universities should assign young Chinese international students with a lower level of English proficiency to take English as a second language (ESL) courses before allowing them to take in the regular academic courses.

Limitations and Future Study

Several limitations were involved in this study. First, participants in this study were recruited from two universities which may not represent the whole Chinese international student population in the US. Therefore, future research should consider conducting a national survey to involve a larger population of the young Chinese international students. Additionally, the Cronbach's alpha of self-perception is relatively low in this study which may not well represent the results. As a result, more research is needed in the future to confirm or refute the findings. In terms of future study, it is necessary to consider factors such as gender, year of studying in the US, and majors when analyzing the relationship of academic stresses and their predictive factors. Finally, a mixed-method study could be considered, which would provide an opportunity to explore a more in-depth discovery of the relationship of young Chinese international students' academic stresses, emotional well-being, English proficiency, and social support they receive.

References

Alharbi, Eman S., and Andrew P. Smith. 2018. "Review of the Literature on Stress and Wellbeing of International Students in English-speaking Countries." *International Education Studies* 11: 22-44.

Bai, Jieru. 2016. "Perceived Support as a Predictor of Acculturative Stress among International Students in the United States." *Journal of International Students* 6:93-106.

Banjong, Delphine N. 2015. "International Students' Enhanced Academic Performance: Effects of Campus Resources." *Journal of International Students* 5:132-142.

Barclay, Rachel T., Mandie Weinandt, and Allen C. Barclay. 2017. "The Economic Impact of Study Abroad on Chinese Students and China's Gross Domestic Product." *Journal of Applied Business and Economics,* 19: 30-36.

Barron, Paul, Tom Baum, and Fiona Conway. 2007. "Learning, Living and Working: Experiences of International Postgraduate Students at a Scottish University." *Journal of Hospitality and Tourism Management* 14: 85-101. doi:10.1375/jhtm.14.2.85.

Bevis, Teresa. 2002. "At a Glance: International Students in the United States." *International Educator* 11:12–17.

Brauss, Minerva R., Xi Lin, and Barbara A. Baker. 2015. "International Students in Higher Education: Educational and Social Experiences." *Institute for Learning Styles Journal* 1:54-71.

Carney-Hall, Karla C. 2008. "Understanding Current Trends in Family Involvement". *New Directions for Student Services* 122: 3-14. doi:10.1002/ss.271.

Chao, Ruth C.-L. 2012. "Managing Perceived Stress among College Wtudents: The Roles of Social Support and Dysfunctional Coping". *Journal of College Counseling* 15:5–21. doi.org/10.1002/j.2161-1882.2012.00002.x.

Chen, Bin-Bin, Nora Wiium, Radosveta Dimitrova, and Ning Chen. 2017. "The Relationships Between Family, School and Community Support and Boundaries and Student Engagement among Chinese Adolescents." *Current Psychology*, 1-10. doi:10.1007/s12144-017-9646-0.

Chen, Yajing, and Heidi Ross. 2015. "Creating a Home Away from Home": Chinese Undergraduate Student Enclaves in US Higher Education." *Journal of Current Chinese Affairs* 44:155-181.

Chirkov, Valery, Maarten Vansteenkiste, Ran Tao, and Martin Lynch. 2007. "The Role of Self-Determined Motivation and Goals for Study Abroad in the Adaptation of International Students." *International Journal of Intercultural Relations* 31:199–222. doi:10.1016/j.ijintrel.2006.03.002

Constantine, Madonna G., Sumie Okazaki, and Shawn O. Utsey. 2004. "Self- Concealment, Social Self- Efficacy, Acculturative Stress, and Depression in African, Asian, and Latin American International College Students." *American Journal of Orthopsychiatry* 74:230-241. doi:10.1037/0002-9432.74.3.230.

Crockett, Lisa J., Maria I. Iturbide, Rosalie A. Torres Stone, Meredith McGinley, Marcela Raffaelli, and Gustavo Carlo. 2007. "Acculturative Stress, Social Support, and Coping: Relations to Psychological Adjustment among Mexican American College Students." *Cultural Diversity and Ethnic Minority Psychology* 13:347-355. doi:10.1037/1099-9809.13.4.347.

Desjardins, Tracy, and Bonnie J. Leadbeater. 2017. "Changes in Parental Emotional Support and Psychological Control in Early Adulthood: Direct and Indirect Associations with Educational and Occupational Adjustment." *Emerging Adulthood* 5:177-190. doi:10.1177/2167696816666974.

Fingerman, Karen L., Yen-Pi Cheng, Eric D. Wesselmann, Steven Zarit, Frank Furstenberg, and Kira S. Birditt. 2012. "Helicopter Parents and Landing Pad Kids: Intense Parental Support of Grown Children." *Journal of Marriage and Family* 74:880-896. doi:10.1111/j.1741-3737.2012.00987.x.

Forbush, Eric, and Brooke Foucault-Welles. 2016. "Social Media Use and Adaptation among Chinese Students Beginning to Study in the United States." *International Journal of Intercultural Relations* 50:1-12. doi:10.1016/j.ijintrel.2015.10.007.

Galchenko, Irina, and Fons J.R. van de Vijver. 2007. "The Role of Perceived Cultural Distance in the Acculturation of Exchange Students in Russia." *International Journal of Intercultural Relations* 31:181–197. doi:10.1016/j.ijintrel.2006.03.004.

Gardiner, Sarah, and Anna Kwek. 2017. "Chinese Participation in Adventure Tourism: A Study of Generation Y International Students' Perceptions." *Journal of Travel Research* 56:496-506. doi:10.1177/0047287516646221.

Hawthorne, Lesleyanne. 2010. "Demography, Migration and Demand for International Students." In *Globalisation and Tertiary Education in the Asia-Pacific: The Changing Nature of a Dynamic Market,* edited by Christopher Findlay and William G. Tierney, 93–119. Hackensack, NJ: World Scientific Publishing.

Hazen, Helen D., and Heike C. Alberts. 2006. "Visitors or Immigrants? International Students in the United States." *Population, Space and Place* 12:201–216. doi:10.1002/psp.409.

Hwang, Wei-Chin, & Julia Y. Ting. 2008. "Disaggregating the Effects of Acculturation and Acculturative Stress on the Mental Health of Asian Students." *Cultural Diversity and Ethnic Minority Psychology* 14:147-154. doi: 10.1037/1099-9809.14.2.147.

Institute of International Education. 2013. *International Student Enrollment Trends, 1948/49-2017/17. Open Doors Report on International Educational Exchange.* Retrieved from http://www.iie.org/opendoors.

Institute of International Education. 2014. *International Student Enrollment Trends, 1948/49-2017/17. Open Doors Report on International Educational Exchange.* Retrieved from http://www.iie.org/opendoors.

Institute of International Education. 2017. *International Student Enrollment Trends, 1948/49-2017/17. Open Doors Report on International Educational Exchange.* Retrieved from http://www.iie.org/opendoors.

King, Brian, and Sarah Gardiner. 2015. "Chinese International Students. An Avant- Garde of Independent Travellers?" *International Journal of Tourism Research* 17:130-139. doi:10.1002/jtr.1971.

Kuo, Ben C. H., and Gargi Roysircar. 2004. "Predictors of Acculturation for Chinese Adolescents in Canada: Age of Arrival, Length of Stay, Social Class and English Reading Ability." *Journal of Multicultural Counseling and Development* 32:143-154.

Liao, Kelly Y. H., and Meifen Wie. 2014. "Academic Stresses and Positive Affect: Asian Value and Self-Worth Contingency as Moderators among

Chinese International Students." *Cultural Diversity and Ethnic Minority Psychology* 20:107-115. doi:10.1037/a0034071.

Liu, Danica W. Y., and Belinda Winder. 2014. "Exploring Foreign Undergraduate Students' Experiences of University." *International Journal of Qualitative Studies in Education* 27:42-64. doi:10.1080/09518398.2012.736643

Mertler, C., & Vannatta, R. 2002. *Statistical methods: Practical application and interpretation* (2nd ed.). Los Angeles, CA: Pyrczak.

Murphy, Kerri A., David L. Blustein, Amanda J. Bohlig, and Melissa G. Platt. 2010. "The College-to-Career Transition: An Exploration of Emerging Adulthood." *Journal of Counseling & Development* 88:174–181. doi:10. 1002/j.1556-6678.2010.tb00006.x.

Murray, Christopher, Allison Lombardi, Franklin W. Bender, and Hilary Gerdes. 2013. "Social Support: Main and Moderating Effects on the Relation Between Financial Stress and Adjustment among College Students with Disabilities." *Social Psychology of Education* 16:277-295. doi:10.1007/s11218-012-9204-4.

Neri, Frank, Simon Ville. 2008. "Social Capital Renewal and the Academic Performance of International Students in Australia." *Journal of Socio-Economics* 37:1515-1538. doi:10.1016/j.socec.2007.03.010.

Rahat, Enes, and Tahsin Ilhan. 2016. "Coping Styles, Social Support, Relational Self-Construal, and Resilience in Predicting Students' Adjustment to University Life." *Educational Sciences: Theory and Practice* 16:187-208. doi:10.12738/estp.2016.1.0058.

Ratelle, Catherine F., Simon Larose, Frederic Guay, and Caroline Senecal. 2005. "Perceptions of Parental Involvement and Support as Predictors of College Students' Persistence in a Science Curriculum." *Journal of Family Psychology* 19:286-293. doi:10.1037/0893-3200.19.2.286.

Salami, Samuel, O. 2011. "Psychosocial Predictors of Adjustment among First Year College of Education Students." *US-China Education Review* 8:239–248.

Sawir, Erlenawati, Simon Marginson, Ana Deumert, Chris Nyland, and Gaby Ramia. 2008. "Loneliness and International Students: An

Australian Study". *Journal of Studies in International Education* 12:148-180. doi:10.1177/10283315307299699.

Shoup, Richard, Robert M. Gonyea, and George D. Kuh. 2009. "Helicopter parents: Examining the impact of highly involved parents on student engagement and educational outcomes." *Paper presented at the 49th Annual Forum of the Association for Institutional Research*, Atlanta, Georgia. Retrieved from http://cpr.iub.edu/uploads/AIR%202009%20Impact%20of%20Helicopter%20Parents.pdf.

Smith, Rachel A., and Nigar G. Khawaja. 2011. "A Review of the Acculturation Experiences of International Students." *International Journal of Intercultural Relations* 35:699–713. doi:10.1016/j.ijintrel.2011.08.004.

Wan, Guofang. 2001. "The Learning Experiences of Chinese Students in American Universities: A Cross-Cultural Perspective." *College Student Journal* 35:28–44.

Wei, Meifen, P. Paul Heppner, Michael J. Mallen, Tsun-Yao Ku, Kelly Yu-Hsin Liao, and Tsui-Feng Wu. 2007. "Acculturative Stress, Perfectionism, Years in the United States, and Depression among Chinese International Students." *Journal of Counseling Psychology* 54:385-394. doi:10.1037/0022-0167.54.4.385.

Yan, Kun, and David C. Berliner. 2013. "Chinese International Students' Personal and Sociocultural Stressors in the United States." *Journal of College Student Development* 54:62–84. doi:10.1353/csd.2013.0010.

Yusoff, Yusliza M., and Abdul K. Othman. 2011. "An Early Study on Perceived Social Support and Psychological Adjustment among International Students: The Case of a Higher Learning Institution in Malaysia." *International Journal of Business & Society* 12:1–15.

Zimet, Gregory D., Nancy W. Dahlem, Sara G. Zimet, and Gordon K. Farley.1988. "The Multidimensional Scale of Perceived Social Support." *Journal of Personality Assessment* 52:30–41. doi:10.1207/s15327752jpa5201_2.

Zucker, Lynne. G., and Darby, Michael. R. 2007. "Star scientists, innovation and regional and national immigration." *NBER Working Paper 13547*. National Bureau of Economic Research, Cambridge, MA. https://www.nber.org/papers/w13547.pdf.

In: Exploring the Opportunities ...
Editor: Michael Allison

ISBN: 978-1-53616-241-7
© 2019 Nova Science Publishers, Inc.

Chapter 4

GREAT EXPECTATIONS OF STUDYING ABROAD: EXCHANGE STUDENTS FROM UMEÅ UNIVERSITY, SWEDEN

Per A. Nilsson[*], *Kerstin Westin and Dieter K. Müller*
Department of Geography, Umeå University, Umeå, Sweden

ABSTRACT

The aim of this study is to investigate students' expectations and experiences when studying abroad. A group of outbound exchange students at Umeå University, Sweden, were surveyed before and after the experience of studying in a foreign country. The study is based on a panel of 57 students, who answered one questionnaire prior to leaving for studies abroad and another after six months when most had returned to Sweden. Overall, the students were satisfied with their stay abroad. While the findings are partly in line with previous studies – the students expected to develop their language skills, learn more about another culture, develop as a person, and use the experience as a merit in their future career – this study also showed that in some aspects their perception of studying abroad changed. Perceptions that changed between the questionnaires concerned

[*] Corresponding Author's Email: per.a.nilsson@umu.se.

courses not being offered at Umeå University, more courses being available abroad than at home, and change of environment; the students appreciated this change more than they had expected. Moreover, the willingness to work abroad after finishing the studies was assessed lower upon the return home after the time abroad. Swedish outbound exchange students can be characterized as participants in horizontal mobility, as they expect a foreign higher education institution (HEI) to be of similar quality as their home university, thus emphasizing personal development more than academic achievement.

Keywords: outbound students, student mobility, experiences and expectations, follow-up, Sweden

INTRODUCTION

International mobility has become a pertinent phenomenon in modern society (OECD 2009; 2013; 2014), and is today discussed by some as a problem in relation to refugees (Ergin, De Wit & Leask 2019) and other groups they regard as unwelcome, and by others as an asset when it comes to tourists and the highly educated (King 2017; Teichler 2017). Particularly access to human capital has been interpreted as an integral part of a constant struggle by regions and places to succeed in a global marketplace (Kotler, Bowen & Makens 2013). A privileged group in this context is that of students seeking international experiences (Lörz, Netz & Quast 2016; Netz & Finger 2016; Kratz & Netz 2018). Since the 1970s, the number of students studying abroad has increased considerably worldwide. For instance, in 2014 approximately 4.5 million students were enrolled in studies outside their country of citizenship, in comparison to 0.8 million in 1975 (OECD 2014). In some parts of the world, higher education has become an important export industry, as international students moving outside formal agreements are expected to pay fees for their education (Beech 2018).

In Europe, the Erasmus Program, funded by the European Union, has boosted international student mobility. Today, more than 200,000 students participate in the program annually (European Commission 2015). A recent figure shows that the annual number of Erasmus students accounts for approximately 5% of all graduates (ibid.) Yet there are more possibilities for outbound students than just the Erasmus Program; for instance, universities have formal agreements with institutions all over the world.

In recent years, the growing student mobility has attracted the attention of social scientists. Studies have addressed patterns of mobility and discussed their value for students (Börjesson 2017; King 2017; Kratz & Netz 2018). Moreover, several studies have examined the outcomes of international student mobility as well as the rationales behind the development of student mobility in global higher education (e.g., Teichle 2017; Roy, Newman, Ellenberger & Pyman 2018). According to Findlay et al. (2006), student mobility can be conceptualized theoretically in three ways: as an element of highly skilled migration, as a product of globalization, and as an element of youth mobility cultures and consumption of a project for pursuing self-realization (Cohen, Duncan & Thulemark 2015). Observing an increase in the number of students studying abroad leads to questions about these students' expectations and how they are being met. Thus, learning more about students' experiences from a period of temporary study in a foreign country is important in order to gain a deeper understanding of mobility among young people regarding different domains in life such as career, employability, living abroad, and other life trajectories.

This study highlights students' rationales for becoming exchange students, and how they report their experiences after having temporarily studied abroad. The aim is to investigate the extent to which their expectations were met after a period as an exchange student, be it for academic purposes or other motives. In other words, measuring the students' experiences from a sojourn abroad might give a better understanding of what constitutes a functional and well-defined exchange program for students. This will be pertinent when communicating with partner universities in regard to existing exchange agreements and for the evaluation process before prolonging agreements. Learning more about what students expect, and matching this with their experiences, is one way of improving the exchange of students between HEIs. Well-received exchange programs among students will likely, in the long run, encourage more students to go abroad to have international experiences.

Previous Studies

In this study, mobility is defined as students moving from one country to another as exchange students. However, it is important to emphasize that mobility is more than simply travelling from one country to another. 'It is about a new hierarchy based on the ways we move and the meanings these movements have been given' (Cresswell 2006, 265). Mobility can be a way to achieve one's lifestyle aspirations and greater life satisfaction (Nilsson & Stålnacke 2019). Life satisfaction is the degree of the individual's subjective appraisal as to whether his or her aspirations and achievements have been accomplished (Jacobsson & Lexell 2013). Studies indicate that international student mobility may have an effect on certain aspects of life satisfaction (Nilsson 2015a; Nilsson & Stålnacke 2019). According to Teichler (2017), student mobility includes upward social mobility, for instance a move from a less economically advanced country to a more economically advanced one where the HEIs are viewed as academically superior. Other students move to an HEI of equal quality, which would be true for many students enrolled in the Erasmus Program. Teichler calls this horizontal mobility. Sheller (2011) argues that mobility addresses many concerns of contemporary society, such as refugees and border politics, with complex relational dynamics. Hence, in total, only a small share of people are involved in international mobility related to higher education. This is a privileged group, standing in strong contrast to those who lack the means to move (Cresswell 2006; Kmiotek-Meier et al. 2019).

Drawing on Findlay et al. (2006; 2012), the following sections describe three different views on what student mobility represents and how this particular form of mobility can be understood.

Highly Skilled Migration

Many studies identify an interest in cultural experiences as a major reason students choose to temporarily study abroad (Thissen & Ederveen 2006; Roy et al. 2018), while other studies emphasize an improvement in students' human capital and frame it within the context of highly skilled migration (e.g., Findlay, et al., 2006; Findlay et al. 2012). Today, students can participate in mobility with less investment of time and an ability to travel greater distances (Frändberg 2008). However, the length of the study period abroad has been seen as an important delimitation, separating international students into two groups, since the motives for program students coming to Europe to study for a whole degree are somewhat different from those of exchange students who enroll in a mobility program such as Erasmus (Thissen & Ederveen 2006). This has to do with differences in expectations regarding experiences and career. International program students studying for a whole degree, who often pay a fee, are investing a great deal of money in a career, whereas exchange students are focusing on aspects of personal development (Thiessen & Ederveen 2006; Papatsiba 2005).

Previous studies show different outcomes of international student mobility. Studies by Maiworm and Teichler (1996) showed that Erasmus students found work that allowed them to exploit the special skills they had gained during their experience of studying abroad. Norris and Gillespie (2009) found that studying abroad truly changed lives, as the respondents' career choices were affected by the experience. Their study showed that studying abroad affected the career choices of nearly two-thirds of the respondents. In addition, Norwegian mobile students more frequently had jobs with international work assignments (Wiers-Jenssen 2008). And a study by Bracht et al. (2006) reported that while former Erasmus students could not count on higher income and status than their immobile peers, they were finding employment in internationally operating companies and, moreover, were often internationally mobile after graduation. Only former Erasmus students from Central and Eastern European countries could generally expect better career opportunities than their immobile peers (ibid.). Thus, it seems as if the experience of studying abroad has an impact on career choices later in life. In addition, graduates who have experienced international mobility receive higher wages at labor market entry (Kratz & Netz 2018). A study on obstacles to intra-European mobility revealed great divergence between educational and work-related mobility, underlining the diversity included in mobility and a need for tailor-made supporting structures and regulations (Kmoitek-Meier et al. 2019).

Globalization

As Findlay et al. (2012, 120) note, globalization is a complicated term: 'At a more profound level it can signify a more complex range of geopolitical and cultural processes involved in transforming the spatial organization of educational and social relations'. In the context of higher education, this implies that educational systems are globalized, creating global understandings of desirable higher education institutions. This is further supported by a withdrawal of state subsidies causing greater diversity among universities, and consequently a decreasing trust in the state's ability to guarantee a high-class education. The consequence of such an unevenness within the higher education sector is that students with sufficient funds tend to optimize their education outcomes on a global education market (Frändberg 2009; Staniscia 2012). However, far from all students are able to participate in such practice and, thus, some are satisfied with acquiring an education that differs from that of their peers in their home country. A majority, however, will be unaware of or unconcerned with this, and will continue pursuing an education that will lead them into the lower-paying segments of the labor market (Findlay et al. 2012). The authors conclude that the youth of the higher social class reproduces its status through the consumption of education at international high-esteem universities. This has also led to a hierarchical stratification of university systems. Finally, they note that student mobility is of course embedded in wider mobility biographies, in which international trajectories are considered favorable (Waters 2006; Frändberg 2008; 2014). For example, studies by Netz and Finger (2016) indicate that students from a high social class background spend more time abroad than students from a low social class background do.

Youth Cultures and Consumption

For many young people in Western countries, travel entails an adventure as well as an expression of youth mobility cultures and consumption geographies; and, according to Jonsson (2003), why, how, and where you travel says something about who you are and who you want to be. In her Swedish study, Jonsson examined attitudes towards studying abroad among those considering studying at a college or university. The study confirmed findings by, e.g., Bracht et al. (2006), Waters et al. (2010) and CIMO et al. (2013), with the motives given including, for example, the desire to learn a new language or learn about another culture. Jonsson also pointed out some unexpected findings, for instance that the students wanted a break from the monotony of the daily grind, a bit of time to breathe freely, to do something new, and to get away for a while. Moreover, the study showed that young people have highly positive associations regarding internationalization, with many of the respondents wanting to live, work and/or study outside Sweden (ibid.). Temporary mobility can also be seen as a step towards adulthood, and in this context temporary mobility is not necessarily about investing in one's own career but rather postponing long-term decisions (Frändberg 2015). Often, the pressure to succeed is applied by parents rather than the mobile group itself (ibid.)

Similarly, Carlsson (2011), studying German mobile degree students in other European countries, saw international student mobility as a process among young students for becoming mobile, rather than as a distinct and conscious decision to study abroad. Carlsson arrived at the conclusion that students simply become geographically mobile as an outcome of different social and long-term biographical processes and events, i.e., being part of a youth mobility culture. For some, international student mobility is perceived as a means to travel to other countries, and for others as a means to achieve interesting and challenging academic studies at another HEI. However, some enjoy both aspects and it should be recognized that there can be a mix of rationales.

Even though international student mobility has grown since the 1970s, it has not attained the scale anticipated, considering the various possibilities students at HEIs have for studying abroad. It is obvious that most students are non-mobile, with only approximately 2% or slightly more of all students around the world studying abroad (Teichler 2017). Some scholars emphasize that the social 'elite' have the most to gain when it comes to international student mobility (Börjesson 2005; Gribble 2008; Netz & Finger 2016).

A Swedish Perspective

Mobility practices are certainly also culturally embedded and, thus, the inclination and ability to engage in international studies differ between countries depending on, among other things, the status of the national education system and the individual ability to fund the studies. Sweden is among the European countries that obviously provide a context with low enrolment figures for international exchange programs (CIMO et al. 2013).

To date, few studies have addressed the Swedish situation in particular, but the issue has engaged public authorities and not least the Swedish Higher Education Authority (UKÄ). One study, however, showed that the share of outbound students having parents with a least three years of post-secondary education was 49%, compared to 39% of the total student population (UKÄ 2016). Sweden is an Anglophone country (King et al. 2010), meaning that outbound students are looking for study opportunities in English-speaking countries and, furthermore, that inbound students can study in English in non-English-speaking countries. This makes the students biased in relation to the English-speaking world, as many HEIs in non-English-speaking countries can only offer a limited number of courses taught in English. Thus, the place of study is pertinent for some students in relation to studying abroad. Not only does the importance of place distinguish mobile students from non-mobile students; the international experience also places students within a mobility hierarchy (Prazeres 2018). International student mobility is an important part of many students' life planning, and studying abroad is not only a way to receive a formal education. According to students, it is more about being part of a wider process including socially and culturally constructed knowledge, producing a global hierarchy of HEIs (Teichler

2017). In Sweden, as in many other countries, international student mobility is politically encouraged (SOU 2018:3). There is a political consensus that student mobility is an asset in a global knowledge-based economy, and is beneficiary to students as well as the nation state (ibid.). Students have many options in regard to studying abroad. Still, this choice is not utilized among the vast majority of students; as mentioned, some studies indicate social differentiation in Swedish student mobility in relation to the level of education among the parents of outbound students (UKÄ 2016).

METHODS AND DATA

A common problem with measuring students' various motivations to study abroad is the timing of such assessments. Stated preferences prior to departure may romanticize the outcomes of studying abroad, while ex-post evaluations may tend to provide rationales that had not been there prior to departure. Hence, in this study an approach has been chosen that attempts to account for change by combining questionnaires prior to and after a period of studying abroad. This allows for not only the comparison of certain aspects before and after being abroad, but also the assessment of any change that may have occurred.

Participants

The study, based on a questionnaire survey directed at outbound exchange students during the 2007/2008 academic year, is part of a comprehensive study covering in- and outbound students (Nilsson 2015a; Nilsson 2015b; Nilsson & Stålnacke 2019). Initially, 143 students from Umeå University (a university in northern Sweden with 32,000 students) who were enrolled in an exchange program in the autumn term of 2007 were approached. Of these, 123 had signed up for one semester at a university abroad and the remaining 20 were to spend a full academic year abroad.

Two-thirds were Erasmus students, while the others were bound for studies in North America and Australia.

Before leaving to study abroad, the 143 outbound students received a web-based questionnaire. The questionnaire contained questions about their previous experiences of travelling and living abroad, motives for enrolling in an international study program, choice of study destination, and expectations (such as learning another language, getting to know another country and culture, fulfilling a sense of adventure, etc.). A seven-point Likert scale was used in the survey for statements concerning the motives and expectations for, and the outcomes of, the study period abroad. The scale ranged from 1 (do not agree) to 7 (fully agree).

The response rate was 56% (n = 80). When returning from the study period abroad, these 80 students received a follow-up questionnaire. Most of the questions were identical to those in the first questionnaire, but the second one also included a number of questions relating to the outcome. Of the 62 students who answered the second questionnaire, 57 could be matched and linked to the previous one. The panel therefore encompasses 40% of the population of 143 outbound students.

The panel is representative of the students' answers to the first questionnaire, with the exception of a slight overrepresentation of women in the panel. In the first survey 59% of the respondents were women, while in the panel women constitute 65% (see Table 1). In both the first questionnaire and the panel, the respondents were an average of 24 years old, 90% had grown up in Sweden, and a majority were studying within the Social Sciences.

The data set in the analysis consists of the 57 students who answered both questionnaires. Paired sample T-tests have been used when comparing the two samples. Chi square tests have been used to measure associations between sub-groups. All statistical analyses were performed using SPSS, version 17.0 for Windows. The level of statistical significance was set to $p < 0.05$.

Table 1. Respondents' characteristics for the two questionnaires

	Respondents to first questionnaire n = 80	The panel (respondents to both questionnaires) n = 57
Gender		
Female	47 (59%)	37 (64.9%)
Male	33 (41%)	20 (35.1%)
Mean age	24.06 ±2.9	24.09 ±3.3
Upbringing		
Sweden	71 (89%)	51 (90%)
Abroad	9 (11%)	6 (10%)
Lived a period in a foreign country before studying abroad		
Yes	40 (50%)	28 (49%)
No	40 (50%)	29 (51%)
Field of studies		
Humanities	2 (2.5%)	2 (3.5%)
Social Sciences (incl. Law & Business)	60 (75%)	41 (71.9%)
Teacher Training	3 (3.8%)	2 (3.5%)
Natural Sciences/Technology	9 (11.3%)	7 (12.3%)
Medicine, Odontology and Healthcare	4 (5.0%)	3 (5.3%)
Art and Fine Arts	2 (2.5%)	2 (3.5%)
Length of studies abroad		
One semester	71 (89%)	54 (95%)
Two semesters	9 (11%)	3 (5%)

RESULTS

Students' Background

The majority of the respondents (90%) had grown up in Sweden and, as expected, had very good proficiency in Swedish, although a few reported slightly lower proficiency despite having grown up in Sweden. English is mandatory in Swedish schools from the third grade, which was reflected in a high degree of proficiency in English. Furthermore, half of the panel reported having lived for a period in a foreign country before the experience studying abroad, which had given them an opportunity to practice languages. There were no significant differences in proficiency between men and women, or between students in different degree programs.

The respondents' main destinations were English-speaking countries: 19 had studied in the UK, while ten had chosen the US or Canada. Europe was the most frequently chosen geographical area, with 39 respondents having studied in the UK, Germany, France, Spain, or other European countries. However, language proficiency correlates to some degree with the choice of destination. Students who had chosen a non-English-speaking country such as Germany, France, Japan, China or Lithuania also reported a proficiency in these languages.

Destination

About half (32) of the respondents in the panel had chosen to study in an English-speaking country. Those who went to a non-English-speaking country had more experience living abroad for some period in their life, compared to those who chose an English-speaking destination ($p < 0.05$). Of the 25 students who studied in a non-English-speaking country, 17 had lived abroad for some period in their life, compared to 11 of the 25 students who chose an English-speaking destination. The existence of an agreement between the home university and the host university was the most important reason for the choice of destination. As Figure 1 shows, the mean assessment was 5.8 on the seven-point Likert scale, and almost half of the respondents marked a 6 or 7 on the scale. Recommendations from friends or teachers were less important for the choice of destination. However, for three out of four students, the place was more important than the HEI itself when choosing the destination.

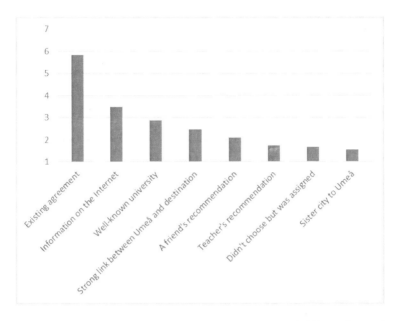

Figure 1. The choice of study destination and the importance of different issues for making the choice. (Assessments were made on a seven-point scale, where 1 = do not agree, and 7 = fully agree.

Expectations and Outcome

The respondents had a positive attitude regarding studying abroad (Figure 2). They agreed that universities should facilitate for those wishing to study abroad, that it is positive when young people go abroad, and that it is important to get student loans. They did not agree that it is up to the individual to arrange their studies abroad, that transferring credits is hard, or that studying abroad is overrated. There was significant difference in attitudes before leaving and after returning home on the issues 'exciting to live abroad' and 'study loans do not cover the expenses'. It is important, though, to once again recognize the selectivity in the sample: the respondents had made the decision to go abroad, and had they been negative to the idea they most likely would not have made this decision.

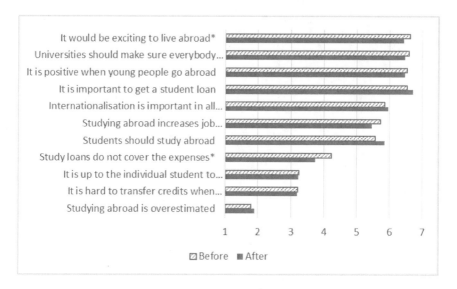

Figure 2. General attitudes towards studying abroad. (Paired-samples T-test. Assessments were made on a seven-point scale, where 1 = do not agree, and 7 = fully agree.).

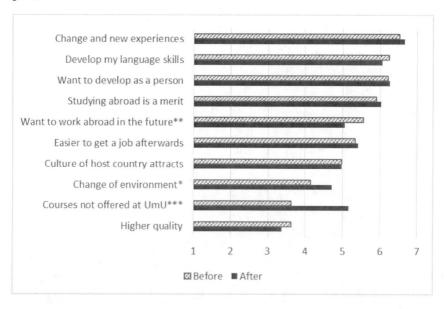

Figure 3. Expectations and outcome of a study period abroad. (Paired-samples T-test. Assessments were made on a seven-point scale, where 1 = do not agree, and 7 = fully agree.).

The students' expectations can partly be described as their motives for studying abroad. Their expectations for the study period abroad were largely fulfilled. They had wanted a change of environment and new experiences, to develop their language skills, and to develop personally, and these expectations were fulfilled (see Figure 3). One expectation that was exceeded was that there were more courses offered at the destination that were not available at Umeå University. Conversely, the desire to work abroad in the future was lower after returning home. Men and women made similar assessments, with the only significant difference being that women to a higher degree than men had found that there were more courses available that could not be found at Umeå University. Being an outbound Swedish exchange student is something one participates in voluntarily, and students who do this are therefore highly motivated. This might explain why many of the respondents' opinions had not changed after their experience of studying in a foreign country.

As has been shown in this section, most of the students' expectations were fulfilled. Before departing as an exchange student, the majority of the respondents had an expectation of excitement and adventure, and of the ability to take advantage of the opportunity to study abroad as regards academic and personal exploration. Important elements seem to be developing language skills, learning more about another culture, developing as a person, and using the experience as a merit in one's future career. Many students expected the merit of having studied abroad to help them find a job more easily. This study indicates that their expectations were met, and that they were very satisfied with their overall experience of temporarily studying abroad.

DISCUSSION

The starting point for this article was to explore a theoretical framework by Findlay et al. (2006; 2012): conceptualizing international student mobility as high-skilled migration; globalization; and youth cultures and consumption. This study is limited to outbound exchange students and discusses within a broader framework placing international student mobility within a context. The survey questions are only related to some of the issues discussed in this section, but are relevant when aiming to understand the degree to which students' expectations are met after a sojourn abroad .

High-skilled migration. It is noteworthy that half of the respondents reported having lived abroad for a period in a foreign country before the experience of studying abroad. They had experience of residing abroad, being part of another culture and managing a foreign language, which might make them more open to studying abroad. At the same time, the desire to actually live abroad decreased after the experience of being an outbound exchange student. As Teichler (2017) pointed out, the vast majority of exchange students do not expect a higher level of teaching or substance of knowledge taught when deciding to study abroad. They have other aims, such as living in another country, exploring a new culture, and achieving personal development. However, an international experience can serve as a door-opener for career opportunities in the country where the student has studied (Teichler 2002; 2004), i.e., leading to issues of youth cultures and consumption. Students are often met with 'political' arguments as motivation to participate in an international student mobility program, for instance as expressed in the Erasmus Program, such as bringing young university students together for mutual learning and understanding. Young people value being able to choose their life path and lifestyle (Frändberg 2015), and it seems clear that personal rationales need to be emphasized and met to encourage studying abroad. Stretwieser et al. (2012) argue for more in-depth research to more fully understand the study-abroad experience. As this study shows, there is a mixture of motives for students to take part in studying abroad: to change study environment, to have an adventure, and to have a personal experience. When studying international student mobility from an individual perspective, it is obvious that students have different backgrounds and needs. In the present follow-up study, outbound exchange students were studied in order to draw conclusions from what they had experienced after having temporarily studied abroad . Following the same individuals over time, it is possible to learn more about how their perspectives changed and how they viewed the experience of studying abroad before and after actually having had the experience. In order to expect something, you first need knowledge about what to expect. Studying abroad is a process that changes a student's perspectives and does something to them as a person. Mobility among students has allowed for increased understanding between different cultures and nations, which has also proven to be important for finding work in international businesses and organizations (Wiers-Jenssen 2008; 2013).

Globalization. The globalization of post-secondary education has led to greater possibilities for students wanting to study abroad, due to an integration of curricula across borders and the increased international exchange of students. The Swedish outbound students in this study participated in international student mobility voluntarily; they had made a choice to become an outbound exchange student, and were highly motivated to temporarily study abroad. After their semester abroad, they returned to finish a degree. Studies on Swedish outbound students show that English-speaking destinations and/or HEIs with many courses taught in English are popular with them (King et al. 2010; UKÄ 2016). A prerequisite for all exchange students is the existence of agreements with partner universities around the world. Thus, the choices exchange students make when it comes to study destinations are within the framework of an agreement. It is obvious that the choices students can make entail a limited choice and, furthermore, these formal networks only exist at the institution where they are currently studying. Still, students seem to appreciate the support they receive in this decision process. The students in this study did not agree that the arrangements for facilitating studying abroad are solely up to the individual student but rather believed this should be a major concern for the HEIs. Students are different: some are self-confident and intellectual explorers attracted by study destinations far from Sweden, while others, perhaps less experienced travelers, look for options closer to home. Nevertheless, students' choices of study destination are interesting to scrutinize and do not depend on existing networks alone. Students have personal preferences, which often involve aspects outside the domain of academia. Sometimes their preferences can be met by the HEI, but not always, especially when the students want to reach out and explore the world and all its diversity.

According to Findlay et al. (2006), Swedish outbound students seem to fit into the category of 'youth mobility culture' pursuing self-realization, as they have travelled to a good number of countries before becoming an exchange student. On many occasions the students become geographically mobile simply because they have a desire to study and work internationally, and their peers as well as the HEI somehow expect them to participate. However, later in life the experience of studying abroad can lead to further mobility choices to work and live abroad in order to improve career opportunities and satisfaction with life; and, indeed, already during their stay abroad they start to appreciate the competence benefits they gain by attending courses not available at their home university. The possibilities for migration are greater for a person with diverse skills than for someone with fewer skills. The ability to reach out to a 'borderless' labor market is attractive (ibid.).

For most exchange students, studying abroad is a short-term event that can be described as participating in a youth mobility culture and as horizontal mobility, in the sense that the students expect the foreign study destination to be more or less equal to the HEI at home (Teichler 2017). This seems to also be true for Swedish outbound students. It should be emphasized that something that is a motive for studying abroad for some students might be an obstacle for others. Nevertheless, students are expected by policymakers (e.g., the Erasmus Program, financed by the EU) to take advantage of the opportunity to study abroad when it comes to academic and personal exploration. An important element seems to be to connect with peers from other countries and to learn more about another culture. An additional issue can involve how international students are taken care of upon arrival, and during their period of study, at a foreign HEI. A well-organized mentor/peer/buddy Program can offer international students a great deal of social activities that they are content with. However, a well-developed social support program can make the students stay with the program and thereby miss opportunities to mix with national students outside the buddy program. The results from a study by Nilsson (2019) indicate that Umeå University has been more successful with social activities than with opening doors to integrating with national students.

Students who choose to study abroad are taking a significant step in setting in motion their own individual life projects, and it can be assumed that they dream of and aspire to have a great experience, be it for academic or personal development.

This study of Swedish outbound students surveying expectations, previous experience of travelling, etc., relied on a relatively small group of students, who were followed up after a relatively short period of time. Additionally, this study lacks a control group of students studying on campus. The conclusions that can be drawn from follow-up studies depend on the size of the population studied, which may explain why results from follow-up studies can differ. Consequently, of course, this implies that the conclusions mainly apply to the population studied.

Conclusion

Before departing as exchange students, the majority had positive expectations, which were largely fulfilled. The findings in this study indicate that a period of studying abroad enriches students' lives. An international experience can be obtained in many different ways; some study abroad while others travel the world, for instance as backpackers. However, it seems as if internationally experienced students are attracted to enrolling in student mobility programs, which underlines the embeddedness of international student mobility in wider international life trajectories (Frändberg 2008; 2014). It is clear that these students see exchange programs as an opportunity for exploration, but also as a way to use the experience as a merit later in life. Furthermore, the experiences made the students less willing to work outside Sweden, which is interesting considering the wider expectations of international higher education to serve as a tool to prepare people for global labor markets. This unexpected outcome might be explained in the answers to the survey questions about life satisfaction indicating lower levels of somatic and psychological health, as well as satisfaction with life as a whole and contacts with friends while studying abroad (Nilsson 2015a).

In this study, it was found that the students place very high value on their choice of country in which to study. For three of four respondents, when choosing the place to study the destination was more important than the HEI itself. Thus, for most students, the country is more important than the university itself, and this study indicates that the respondents value the study destination more than the HEI. Some studies have shown that international mobility for study purposes may be tied to future intentions concerning places of work and residence (OECD 2009).

Finally, this paper deals with following up on the experiences and outcomes of temporarily studying in a foreign country. It is quite obvious that students have expectations before enrolling in a student mobility program; other scholars have also designed studies to follow up on students' experiences of temporarily studying abroad (Bracht et al. 2006; Campbell & Lee 2008; McLeod & Wainwright 2009). There are few examples of studies following the same individuals from travelling abroad to having actually gained experience of studying at a foreign HEI (Roy et al. 2018), which opens for more comprehensive follow-up studies to learn more about international student mobility. However, outcomes can be difficult to evaluate, depending on when the follow-up studies take place; they can be conducted immediately after a period abroad or up to several years later. It can also depend on whether the studies target exchange students (often Erasmus) or international students in general. According to Teichler (2017), the impacts and outcomes of studying abroad need more attention.

FUTURE RESEARCH

This study has highlighted not only the rationales students have for becoming exchange students but also, most importantly, how they value this experience. A global lifestyle among young people, and the fact that being mobile has become 'normal' among a large group of European university students, also raises questions about the students who are non-mobile, as we know that exchange studies have not attained the scale anticipated by policymakers such as the European Commission. Are students who are not presently attracted to exchange programs already experienced travelers with extensive international practice? Are non-mobile students already participating in global exchange by other means, such as information and communication technologies? Are students more attracted to choosing more freely, outside mobility programs, to have an international experience based on their own preferences and choices?

REFERENCES

Beech, S. E. 2018. "Adapting to change in the higher education system: international student mobility as a migration industry." *Journal of Ethnic and Migration Studies,* 44(4), 610-625. doi: 10.1080/1369183X.2017.1315515.

Bracht O., Engel C., Janson K., Over A., Schomburg H., & Teichler U. 2006. *"The Professional Value of ERASMUS Mobility. Final Report of the VALERA project."* International Centre for Higher Education Research (INCHER-Kassel), University of Kassel, Kassel, Germany.

Börjesson, M. 2005. *Transnationella utbildningsstrategier vid svenska lärosäten och bland svenska studenter i Paris och New York.* [*Transnational education strategies at Swedish universities and among Swedish students in Paris and New York*]. Uppsala University, Sweden. (Doctoral thesis Department of Education).

Börjesson, M. 2017. "The global space of international students in 2010." *Journal of Ethnic and Migration Studies,* 43:8, 1256-1275. http://dx.doi.org/10.1080/1369183X.2017.1300228.

Campbell, J., & Li, M. 2008. "Asian Students Voice: An Empirical Study of Asian Students Learning Experiences at a New Zealand University." *Journal of Studies in International Education*, 12(4), 375-396. https://doi.org/10.1177/1028315307299422.

Carlsson, S. 2011. "Just a Matter of Choice? Student Mobility as a Social and Biographical Process." University of Sussex. *Sussex Centre for Migration Research. Working Paper No 68.*

CIMO (Centre for International Mobility), UHR (Swedish Council for Higher Education) and SIU (Norwegian Centre for International Cooperation in Education).2013. *Living and learning – exchange studies abroad. A study of motives, barriers and experiences of Finnish, Norwegian and Swedish students.* Retrieved from : http://www.cimo.fi/instancedata/prime_product_julkaisu/cimo/embeds/cimowwwstructure/28083_Living_and_learning.pdf.

Cohen, S., A., Duncan, T. & Thulemark, M. 2015. "Lifestyle mobilities: The crossroads of travel, leisure and migration." *Mobilities,* 10 (1), 155-172. doi: 10.1080/17450101.2013.826481.

Cresswell, T. 2006. *On the move. Mobility in the Modern Western World.* Routledge, New York, USA.

Duncan, T., Scott, D. S. & Bauman, T. 2013. "The mobility of hospitality work: an exploration of issues and debates". *Annals of Tourism Research.* Vol 41, 1-19. doi: 10.1016/j.annals.2012.10.004.

Ergin H, Hans de W & Leask, B. 2019. "Forced Internationalization of Higher Education: An Emerging Phenomenon." *International Higher Education* 97: 9-10. doi: http://dx.doi.org/10.6017/ihe.2019.97.10938.

European Commission. 2015. *Erasmus, facts, figures and trends. The European Union support for student and staff exchange and university cooperation in 2013-2014.* Retrieved from: http://ec.europa.eu/education/library/statistics/erasmus-plus-facts-figures_en.pdf.

Findlay, A. M., King, R., Stam, A., & Ruiz-Gelices, E. 2006. "Ever Reluctant Europeans: The Changing Geographies of UK Students Studying and Working Abroad." *European Urban and Regional Studies,* 13(4), 291-318. https://doi.org/10.1177/0969776406065429.

Findlay, A. M., King, R., Geddes, A., Smith, F. M., Geddes, A., and Skeldon, R. 2012. "World class? An investigation of globalization, difference and international student mobility." *Transactions of the Institute of British Geographers.* NS, 118-131. doi10.1111/j.1475-5661.2011.00454.x.

Frändberg, L. 2008. "Paths in transnational time- space: Representing mobility biographies of young Swedes". *Geografiska Annaler: Series B,*

Human Geography, 90(1), 17-28. https://doi.org/10.1111/j.1468-0467.2008.00273.x.

Frändberg, L. 2009. "How normal is travelling abroad? Differences in transnational mobility between groups of young Swedes." *Environment and Planning A*, 41(3), 649-667. https://doi.org/10.1068/a40234.

Frändberg, L. 2014. "Temporary transnational youth migration and its mobility links". *Mobilities*, 9(1), 146-164. https://doi.org/10.1080/17450101.2013.769719.

Frändberg, L. 2015. "Acceleration or avoidance? The role of temporary moves abroad in the transition to adulthood." *Population, Space and Place*, 21(6), 553-567. doi: 10.1002/psp.1851.

Gribble, C. 2008. "Policy options for managing international student migration: the sending country's perspective." *Journal of Higher Education Policy and Management*, 30(1), 25-39. doi: 10.1080/13600800701457830.

Jacobsson, L. & Lexell, J. 2013 "Life satisfaction 6–15 years after a traumatic brain injury." *Journal of Rehabilitation Medicine* 45(10) 1010–1015. https://doi.org/10.2340/16501977-1204.

Jonsson, G. 2003. *Rotad, rotlös, rastlös [Rooted, rootless, and restless]*, GERUM 2003:3 (Doctoral thesis Department of Geography, Umeå University Press, Sweden).

King, R., & Ruiz-Gelices, E. 2003. "International Student Migration and the European `Year Abroad´: Effects on European Identity and Subsequent Migration Behaviour." *International Journal of Population Geography*, 9(3), 229-252. https://doi.org/10.1002/ijpg.280.

King, R., Findlay, A. & Ahrens, J. 2010. *International student mobility literature review*. Reported to HEFCE, and cofounded by the British Council, UK National Agency for Erasmus.

King, R. 2017. "Theorising new European youth mobilities." *Population Space and Place*. 1-12. doi.org/10.1002/psp.2117.

Kmiotek-Meier, E., Skrobanek, J., Nienaber, B., Vysotskaya, V., Samuk, S., Ardic, T., Pavlova, I., Dabasi-Halázs,-Z., Diaz, C., Bissinger, J., Schlimbach, T. & Horvath,K. 2019. "Why is it so hard? And for whom?

Obstacles to intra-European mobility." *Migration Letters* 16(1) 31-44. doi: https://doi.org/10.33182/ml.v16i1.627.

Kotler, P., Bowen, J. & Makens, J. 2013. *Marketing for hospitality and tourism.* Pearson education, Inc. Upper Saddle River.

Kratz, F. & Netz, N. 2018. "Which mechanisms explain monetary returns to international student mobility?" *Studies in Higher Education.* 43:2 375-400. doi: 10.1080/03075079.2016.1172307.

Lörz, M. Netz, N. & Quast, H. 2016. "Why do students from underprivileged families less often intend to study abroad?" *Higher Education* 72:153-174. doi 10.1007/s10734-015-9943-1.

Maiworm, F., & Teichler, U. 1996. *"Study Abroad and Early Career."* London and Bristol, Kingsley.

McLeod, M., & Wainwright, P. 2009. "Researching the Study Abroad Experience". *Journal of Studies in International Education,* 13(1), 66-71. https://doi.org/10.1177/1028315308317219.

Netz, N. & Finger, C. 2016. "New Horizontal Inequalities in German Higher Education? Social Selectivity of Studying abroad between 1991 and 2012." *Sociology of Education* 89(2) 79-98. https://doi.org/10.1177/0038040715627196.

Nilsson, P. A. 2015a. "Life satisfaction among outbound students in northern Sweden." *World Journal of Education.* 5(4) 87-92. doi:10.5430/wje.v5n4p87.

Nilsson, P. A. 2015b. "Expectations and experiences of inbound students: perspectives from Sweden." *Journal of International students* 5(2) 161–174.

Nilsson, P. A. & Stålnacke, B. M. 2019. "Life satisfaction among inbound university students in northern Sweden." *Fennia - International Journal of Geography* 197(1) x–x. https://dx.doi.org/10.11143/fennia.70337.

Nilsson, P. A.2019. *The Buddy Programme - Integration and social support for international students* (submitted manuscript).

Norris, E. M., & Gillespie, J. 2009. "How study Abroad Shapes Global Careers: Evidence From the United States." *Journal of Studies in International Education,* 13(3), 382-397. https://doi.org/10.1177/1028315308319740.

OECD. 2009. *Education at a Glance 2009: OECD Indicators.* Organisation for Economic Co-operation and Development (OECD) Publishing. Retrieved from: http://www.oecd-ilibrary.org/education/education-at-a-glance-2009_eag-2009-en.

OECD. 2013. *Education at a Glance 2013 OECD Indicators.* Organisation for Economic Co-operation and Development (OECD) Publishing. Retrieved from: http://www.oecd-ilibrary.org/education/education-at-a-glance-2013_eag-2013-en.

OECD. 2014. *Education at a Glance 2014: OECD Indicators.* Organisation for Economic Co-operation and Development (OECD) Publishing. Retrieved from: http://www.oecd.org/edu/Education-at-a-Glance-2014.pdf.

Papatsiba, V. 2005. "Political and Individual Rationales of Student Mobility: a case-study of ERASMUS and a French regional scheme for studies abroad." *European Journal of Education*, 2, 173-188. doi: 10.1111/j.1465-3435.2004.00218.x.

Prazeres, L. 2018. "Unpacking distinction within mobility: social prestige and international students." *Population, Space and Place.* https://doi.org/10.1002/psp.2190.

Roy, A., Newman A., Ellenberger, T. & Pyman A. 2018. "Outcomes of international student mobility programs: a systematic review and agenda for future research." *Studies in Higher Education.* doi: 10.1080/03075079.2018.1458222.

Sheller, M. 2011. "Mobility." *Sociopedia.isa*, doi: 10.1177/205684601163.

Staniscia, B. 2012. "Mobility of students and attractiveness of universities. The case of Sapienza University of Rome." *International Review of Sociology*, 22(2), 245-258. https://doi.org/10.1080/03906701.2012.696967.

SOU. 2018. *"En strategisk agenda för internationalisering. Delbetänkande av utredningen om ökad internationalisering av universitet och högskolor. Statens offentliga utredningar 2018:3."* [A strategic agenda for internationalization. Interim report of the report on increased internationalization of universities and colleges. Government public inquiries 2018: 3].Stockholm, Sweden.

Teichler, U. 2002. *Erasmus in the Socrates program. Findings of an evaluation study.* Bonn, Lemmens, Germany.

Teichler, U. 2004. "Temporary study abroad: the life of Erasmus students." *European Journal of Education*, 39(4), 395-408. https://doi.org/10.1111/j.1465-3435.2004.00193.x.

Teichler, U. 2017. "Internationalisation trends in higher education and the changing role of international student mobility." *Journal of international Mobility*, 1(5), 177-216. https://doi.org/10.3917/jim.005.0179.

Thissen, L., & Ederveen, S. 2006. *Higher Education: Time for coordination on European level? Discussion Paper, No 68* (CPB Netherlands Bureau for Economic Policy Analysis).

UKÄ. 2016. *Swedish Higher Education Authority. Higher Education in Sweden. 2016 Status report.* Stockholm, Sweden.

Waters, J. L. 2006. "Geographies of cultural capital: education, international migration and family strategies between Hong Kong and Canada." *Transactions of the Institute of British Geographers*, 31(2), 179-192. https://doi.org/10.1111/j.1475-5661.2006.00202.x.

Waters, J., & Brooks, R. 2010. "'Vive la Difference?': The 'International' Experience of UK Students Overseas." *Population, Space and Place*, 17(5), pp. 587-578. https://doi.org/10.1002/psp.613.

Wiers-Jenssen, J. 2008. "Does Higher Education Attained abroad Lead to International Jobs?" *Journal of Studies in International Education*, 12(2), pp. 101-130. https://doi.org/10.1177/1028315307307656.

Wiers-Jenssen, J. 2013. "Degree mobility from the Nordic countries: Background and employability." *Journal of Studies in International Education*, 17(4), 471-491. https://doi.org/10.1177/1028315312463824.

In: Exploring the Opportunities ...
Editor: Michael Allison

ISBN: 978-1-53616-241-7
© 2019 Nova Science Publishers, Inc.

Chapter 5

EXPLORING CHALLENGES FACED BY INTERNATIONAL STUDENTS IN COMPUTER SCIENCE PROGRAMS: TOWARDS UNDERSTANDING THE STUDENT PERSPECTIVE

Michael J. Oudshoorn[1],*, *Alison Clear*[2], *Janet Carter*[3], *Leo Hitchcock*[4], *Janice L. Pearce*[5] *and Joseph A. Abandoh-Sam* [6]
[1] High Point University, High Point, NC, US
[2] Eastern Institute of Technology, Auckland, New Zealand
[3] University of Kent, Canterbury, Kent, UK
[4] Auckland University of Technology, Auckland, New Zealand
[5] Berea College, Berea, KY, US
[6] Valley View University, Oyibi, Ghana

Abstract

International students are an important and desirable constituent in most computer science programs, bringing new perspectives into the classroom, diversifying the student population, globalizing the curriculum, broadening the perspective of domestic students, and often generating revenue for the host institution. Each of these characteristics is

---
*Corresponding Author's E-mail: moudshoo@highpoint.edu

desirable and increasingly important in today's highly connected world and job market. Most institutions invest resources in attracting international students and providing support and orientation sessions for them on arrival to help acclimate them to the new environment and to introduce them to other students. Student clubs often provide support groups and social functions to help them meet and make friends with domestic students. However, challenges for international students, and for the faculty teaching them, persist at many institutions despite these efforts to help international students deal with culture shock, differing academic expectations and teaching methods, and different attitudes toward issues such as academic honesty. In this chapter, the authors examine the challenges faced by international students in integrating into computer science programs at various institutions, and explores these challenges and identifies differences in student and faculty perceptions. A survey of over 200 international students studying in four counties was conducted to gain insight into student perceptions of their educational experience.

1. Introduction

International education has the possibility of being a truly transformative experience [1]. In this chapter, the authors examine challenges faced by international students in integrating into computer science programs at various focus institutions, explore those challenges, and seek to clarify the student's perception of their international educational experience through a survey. The authors do not seek to compare international and domestic students, instead focusing on the international student and the perceptions that they hold of their educational experience at their host institution. Several of the authors have been international students themselves, or are faculty members who have immigrated, and hence understand and appreciate the challenges that the students are likely to face.

Challenges are not only faced by the students who travel to the host country to pursue a degree, but also by the faculty and administration at the institutions that teach them. These challenges persist despite the resources invested by institutions to create and provide an inclusive and supporting environment for their international students. Such support comes in many forms including orientation sessions, clubs, social events, advising, and regular meetings with support staff to acclimate the students in their new environment. Faculty at many institutions are not provided any training on the challenges facing international students, or, especially, on their cultural backgrounds and/or norms. As a result, classroom challenges can arise. Often these are born from a cultural misunderstanding, or simply a lack of knowledge of the educational system of the student's home country.

The assumption made by institutions appears to be that the support and cultural training given to the incoming international students is sufficient to fully integrate them into classes and the institutional culture, and that training and educating faculty who work with these students is not necessary. However anyone who has lived in another country will attest that cultural adaptation is not instantaneous since it takes substantial time to fully embrace and understand the adopted country. Abandoning one's home country value system and replacing it with that of the adopted country can take a lifetime. However, many institutions appear to expect international students to essentially accept the culture and value set of the host country immediately.

Many faculty do understand that the cultural shift asked of international students does not take place quickly, and that the differences in educational systems and expectations sometimes creates a stressful experience for the international student. In the classroom, this may manifest itself in a number of ways including lack of attendance, poor performance, lack of participation in class discussions, excessive reliance on tutoring and help sessions, and plagiarism. The challenges and stresses of international education are realized, from the classroom instructor's perspective, as challenges of integrating the international student into the program and helping them to achieve their full potential. Faculty, however, do not have prior knowledge of the students performance and behavior to properly measure the impact the challenges of international education and cultural change has on the student. For example, without knowledge of the students previous study habits and academic performance (which often means understanding the academic rigor and standards of the students home institution), it is impossible to determine if the observed student behavior at the host institution differs from their past behavior and performance at their home institution. A student seen to be struggling may always have been a weak student, and a student skipping classes may always have had a habit of skipping classes. However, the orientation sessions that most international students must complete typically emphasizes the need for class attendance, utilization of resources such as help sessions and tutoring, and the avoidance of plagiarism. Of these, plagiarism is given the most attention in the majority of orientation sessions and it is easy to detect and measure, despite the fact that the nature of plagiarism has changed over time [2]. In this chapter we regard plagiarism as a problem, but consider some cases of plagiarism to potentially be a by-product of the student not being fully integrated into the host country's academic system and culture.

Marsden et al. [3] suggest that the rate of plagiarism does not vary drastically between domestic students and international students. However, in the observation of the majority of the authors international students were caught plagiarizing at a higher rate. There may be several factors for this, including more mature plagiarism practices on behalf of the domestic students, but the apparent percentage of international students caught is reason for alarm since their orientation session explicitly addresses plagiarism. Domestic students usually do not get such an orientation session and need to wait until they take a course such as university seminar to be told explicitly that plagiarism is unacceptable. Therefore, the faculty may make the assumption that international students engaging in plagiarism may do so because of the stresses they are facing. McCabe [4] presents data from Canadian and American universities to show that undergraduate students self report a higher rate of engagement in plagiarism at least once in the previous year than graduate students. The rates for each student group was lower than the perceived rate of plagiarism held by faculty, which raises the question of guilt perception [5]. McCabe, however, does not distinguish between international and domestic students. In this chapter, plagiarism is, in part, regarded as a symptom of the stress related to cultural shift and integration into a new environment. This is in no way intended to trivialize the seriousness of plagiarism [6].

The chapter is organized as follows: Section 2. provides background to the problem, describes the methodology used in this chapter to conduct this exploratory investigation. and provides contextual information of each of the authors' institutions. Section 3. examines cultural issues as previously addressed in the literature, and Section 4. looks at the cultural pressures and challenges the international student faces. Orientation practices and impact are examined in Section 5., and Section 6. discusses the results of a survey of international students to gather insight into their international educational experience and their perceived effectiveness of the orientation process. Section 7. offers some observations, and a conclusion is presented in Section 7.. Section 8. considers some options for future work.

2. Background

Students are studying abroad in increasing numbers and institutions are becoming more global in their focus with many delivering courses or having a campus overseas. This has resulted in over one million students and scholars studying abroad at any one time at institutions of higher education [7], or attending foreign higher education programs in their own country. Many international students have difficulty integrating into their host institution's pedagogy and culture, which is manifested in many ways including (but are not limited to) poor grades, difficulty understanding concepts, difficulty reading and following instructions, failing to seek assistance when needed, and an unwillingness or reluctance to participate in class discussions. It is often difficult to know if such observed behavior or reactions are cultural in origin, the individual's ability or skill level, the individual's personality, or a sign of difficulty integrating into the academic environment. The faculty member simply does not know the student well enough and typically does not have knowledge of the student's academic history and how it compares to that of their performance in the host institution.

One common observable and measurable metric is the amount of academic dishonesty involving international students. The authors have assumed the premise that plagiarism, at least in part, is a symptom of a lack of cultural integration and acceptance of the host country's values. There are many, complex factors that drive a student to plagiarize or cheat in some way, but the belief is that if the international student population were fully integrated into the local culture and education system, then the expectation would be that the incidence of plagiarism and cheating among domestic and international students should be indistinguishable. One element covered by almost all orientation programs for international students is that of the academic environment and the consequential expectations of student behavior. This often includes discussion of an honor code or similar statement of acceptable student behavior and academic honesty. Invariably this includes a discussion on academic integrity, what constitutes plagiarism [8], and how such behavior is not acceptable at the host institution. Hence, one could reasonably argue that examples of plagiarism by international students could be a sign that they are struggling to integrate fully into their host country and institution.

Journalists from the Times newspaper in the UK [9] submitted a Freedom of Information request to all UK universities for information relating to plagiarism. Their analysis of data from 129 institutions revealed that almost 50,000 students were accused of plagiarism in the previous three years, with non-EU students being four times more likely to be caught cheating. 70 institutions provided information relating to nationality of students accused of academic dishonesty with 35% of cases involving international students who make up 12% of the student body. They concluded that fears of a plagiarism epidemic is being fueled disproportionately by foreign students. Some institutions attempt to address plagiarism through education and providing students with knowledge related to academic writing and referencing [10, 11], or copyright awareness [12]. Abukari [13] and the Higher Education Academy [14] have completed comprehensive case studies of plagiarism and collusion amongst the student body, and the University of York has examined ways to reduce plagiarism through assessment design [15]. Sheard and Dick [16, 17, 18], Sheard et al. [19, 20], Awuah [6], and Bamford and Serhiou [21] have examined various dimensions for the causes of, and the means to manage, plagiarism. Academic dishonesty can be handled by managing expectations [22]. Pierce and Zilles have examined the relationship between plagiarism and grades [23].

Specific institutional figures reported by journalists demonstrate that 75% of postgraduate plagiarism cases at Queen Mary University, London, involved international students, with 33% from China, even though international students comprise only 20% of the student body. At Staffordshire University, it was reported that over 50% of plagiarism cases involved international students who make up 5% of the student body. Denisova-Schmidt [24, 25, 26] suggests that there are five cases of alleged cheating per 100 international students, compared to 1 per 100 for domestic students. She also states that in the academic year 2014-15 the Department of Immigration in Australia canceled the visas of more than 9,000 international students due to academic misconduct. She further suggests that many of these students come from cultures with endemic corruption, and many of these countries have an academic culture in which students are expected to repeat the information provided by their teachers rather than reflecting upon it themselves. Denisova-Schmidt [24] observed that international students might face challenges integrating into Western "academic freedom" and thus need time to understand how to work. Tierney and Sabharwal [27, 28] analyze the culture of corruption in the Indian higher education sector and further posit that the challenges for any country facing systemic corruption is that the cultural ethos pervades academic behavior and makes it harder to stamp out cheating.

Based on a survey conducted by Oppong [29], it was observed that approximately 92% of respondents indicated that they were aware of institutional regulations on academic dishonesty. This suggests that orientation programs and faculty syllabi are successfully making students aware of academic dishonesty and how the institution responds to it. Only 31% of respondents, however, rated their understanding of the academic dishonesty policies and regulations as high. The respondents believed that the professors had a better understanding of these regulations than the students ($p¡0.001$ and $p¡0.0001$ respectively). Given the relatively small number of students typically charged with academic dishonesty, it is interesting that approximately 40% of respondents indicated that they had witnessed a fellow student engage in academic dishonesty, but the majority (94%) stated that they did not report these acts. The leading causes of, or excuses for, academic dishonesty include a) the pursuit of good grades, b) a high academic load, and c) the pressure to please family and guardians, especially those financially supporting their endeavors. Typical examples of academic dishonesty included cheating during exams, and the sharing of solutions for assignments and other classwork. Respondents believed that copying the work of a fellow student without their permission was a serious offense but that doing so with their knowledge and permission was not. Faculty often encourage students to use each other as a resource to solve problems, while still doing their own work, as a mechanism to manage large classes and workload. It would appear that many students do not know, or fail to acknowledge, the fine line between helping and cheating.

The language barrier also limits access to social services. In the study by Oppong [29], the majority of the respondents did not speak the language of the host country (Finnish), making it very difficult for the international students to interact and socialize with the domestic students and adjust to the general Finnish way of life. Although the medium of instruction at this institution is English, language barriers still makes it a challenge for international students to assimilate into the host culture. Other challenges identified include misconstruing and misinterpreting non-verbal communications such as facial expressions, body language, gestures, and the like [29]. Berglund and Thota [30] undertook a pilot study using a phenomenographic perspective to understand to what extent Chinese students' understanding of computer science culturally situated within the context of a Swedish university and found similar results.

In a study conducted by Russell et al. [31] of approximately 900 international students studying in Australia, 41% of the international students reported experiencing substantial levels of stress. The cause of this stress included feelings of being homesick, culture shock, and a perception of discrimination. In comparison to domestic students, international students need to pay additional attention and actively devote effort to social integration. The support network familiar to the international student includes their family, friends and social network from their home country, but these are typically not within easy reach to help alleviate the stress levels [7, 32, 33]. Common symptoms of culture shock include absent-mindedness, a feeling of helplessness and a desire for dependence on one's own national group, a delay in learning the local language, excessive concern over drinking water and food, fits of anger over minor issues and frustrations, excessive fear for their safety and well-being, concern over minor pain and health issues, and a terrible longing to be back home [34, 35]. The subsequent impact to the student's learning, especially when also confronted with a new teaching environment, can be significant.

Most of the discussion above attempts to provide an explanation for observed behavior of international students. Nisbett [36] simply points out that Asians and "Westerners" think differently, and hence have different attitudes [37, 38]. Alaoutinen and Smolander [39] even ask if computer science students are different learners. Rosenthal and Jacobsen [40] discuss the Pygmalion effect where higher expectations in the classroom leads to higher performance. Inamori and Analoui [41] found that this effect was also applicable in a non-educational, multi-cultural setting. This is identified as an area of research in psychology and potentially suggests that expecting more from international students in terms of adjusting to the new culture could result in better integration.

The faculty involved in this study, and others informally interviewed, perceive that Oppong's study [29], and the findings of Denisova-Schmidt [24, 25, 26], Tierney and Sabharwal [27, 28], and Russell et al. [31] are accurate. The chapter's authors examined the reasons put forward in the literature, however the results are often specific to a small number or a single source country, or specific to a single host institution. From this data, faculty project results onto other cultures and onto their home institution. Such projections may appear relevant and consistent with observations at the faculty member's institution. There are many reasons any student may engage in plagiarism [21], however, international students have additional pressures based on the cultural gap that they experience.

The purpose of our study was to gain an insight into the students perspective of the challenges they face, and to use this insight to guide more focused future work. The authors conducted an international survey to determine student perceptions of the value and success of orientation programs to address the cultural gap and challenges they face. A variety of source and host countries participated in the survey, discussed in Section 6., to see if the projected perceptions were reasonable. Each institution involved in this chapter provide international students with an orientation program to address several of the aspects raised in the literature. The study focus was the institutions associated with the authors: several diverse institutions in differing countries. Those institutions vary in their type and mission, which in turn incorporates differing assumptions and process structures. Each institution has international students studying within a computer science program with some being at the undergraduate level, others at the postgraduate level, and some having international students at both levels. The number of international students within a program varies from relatively small (approximately 8%) to 100% in some cases. Some programs have international students sourced from several countries from a variety of regions around the world, to programs where all students come from a single source country and predominantly from a single city within that country. Despite the rich variety of institutions represented, each experienced common challenges with integration of students into their programs and classes as well as into the local academic environment and community. Academic faculty at each institution felt that more support was necessary to help the students once they arrived in the host country, however many international students are cost and time conscious and typically try to arrive in the host country as close as possible to the start of the semester.

3. International Student Integration Challenges

In many institutions, the growth in the graduate student body tends to be primarily through international students. The main reasons include the cost and debt already incurred by the students in their undergraduate education [35], as well as government capped domestic growth in some cases. There is an argument that institutions have an obligation to invest in strategies to increase the population of domestic students as this provides more opportunity for cultural integration of international students.

Many institutions face financial pressure to increase international student numbers in order to derive revenue to off-set ever decreasing amounts of public support. Given the benefits international students bring to campus [42], it is important that the challenges of cultural integration [38, 43, 44, 45, 46, 47, 48, 49, 50, 51, 52] are addressed. Ideally, international students academically behave and perform in a manner indistinguishable from domestic students. Failure to integrate fully negatively impacts the international student's performance and limits their potential. Faculty aim to fully integrate and motivate all their students [53].

It is well known that cultural differences impact student performance when studying internationally (for example, [7, 54]). There has also been work [55, 56] that attempts to link cultural attitudes to plagiarism amongst international students. However, these works do not identify the role the host institution plays in addressing or mitigating these challenges. For many institutions, this is addressed through an orientation program that international students are expected to participate in.

A 2016 special issue [57] on the needs, experiences and expectations of international students studying in the United States indicates that the US is the leading destination attracting 26% of all students studying internationally, followed by the United Kingdom (15%), France (11%), Germany (10%), and Australia (8%). Yet, at many US campuses, support services for international students fail to extend much beyond immigration and visa compliance. The significant mismatch in expectations of career advancement prior to enrollment and their experience on campus is one of the key reasons identified by international students regarding their dissatisfaction with US campuses.

In the Netherlands, Rienties et al. [33] conducted a cross-institutional comparison among 958 students at five business schools. It was found that academic adjustment is the main predictor of study-performance for domestic Dutch students, Western international, and Mixed-Western international students and for international students with a non-Western background. Social adjustment was negatively correlated to study-performance.

A project undertaken in Nottingham Trent University [58] found that participation of both native and international students in group projects provided better cross-cultural experience and integration for international students. The same study also found that achievement levels are lower for international students when they lived and worked together as a group without mixing with domestic students. This lack of sharing of cultural experiences results in reduced benefits to all students.

A pilot study of Chinese students studying in Sweden [59, 60] identified differences of both pedagogy and course focus as challenges, while simultaneously developing a deeper sensitivity to cultural differences.

A study of international students from Vietnam identified a) cost of education, b) language barrier, c) cultural differences, and d) being away from home as the major challenges in studying abroad [38].

Another study [57] found that international students reported experiencing barriers to work experience including lack of local networks, lack of confidence in communicating in English, as well as perceived employer discrimination.

In two separate studies, Graham [61] and Johnson [62] found that when English proficiency was relatively low, TOEFL scores could predict academic performance in post-secondary institutions in English-speaking host countries. One study found that English language competency was a key factor in determining how students begin to shape their employability in their first year of postgraduate study at an English-speaking institution [63].

Therefore clear cultural and educational differences between domestic and international students exist no matter where the international student chooses to study. A well-trained and more sympathetic faculty [64] can help international students transition as well as reduce the incidence of plagiarism. Carroll [65] notes that faculty can use ways to deter cheating and that various assessment mechanisms can be used to avoid cheating. Carroll points out that the approach of "catch and punish" drains the faculty of valuable teaching time and students of learning time. Sheard and Dick [16] also show different approaches a faculty could take to minimize cheating in their classes.

4. Cultural Pressure/Challenges

Every country possesses cultural practices that differentiates it from other countries in the world. Even though countries from the same continent or geographical region may be similar, subtle differences between a shared or similar practice may exist [66]. If cultural challenges can present hurdles for individuals from similar cultures who speak the same language, they almost certainly present more significant challenges to relatively young, and culturally diverse international students. A case study of Ghanaian and Nigerian students in Finland [29] found that when international students arrive at their host countries, they come with their belief systems, culture, food preferences, and way of life.

Cultural pressures or challenges amongst international students comes in different forms. Sometimes the challenge can be as small as "missing homemade food" to their inability to express themselves adequately in the language of the host institution. The challenges they face with different living conditions, time management, language and cultural barriers, and different learning styles lead to the transitional difficulties and socio-cultural adaptations. Indeed, food was mentioned by 63.3% of survey respondents as one of the things they missed most from home, with 32.2% listing food exclusively. (see Table 8).

Although most, if not all, host institutions provide international students with orientation on their country's culture, differences in cultural norms and practices still play a significant role in their success in computer science programs as is evident in their academic activities such as group formation and assignments. Abufardeh [67] points out:

> "Cultural differences can occur even when teams share a common language and nationality; differences in 'corporate culture' can lead to conflicting approaches to problem solving and communication, which in turn might be misinterpreted as rudeness or incompetence".

This remains true even after graduation when it comes to professional groups or teams [68].

With regard to academic dishonesty, in some cases, the culture of the source country towards academic dishonesty can be lax, so much so that many international students are unaware of the implications of academic dishonesty [55, 56]. This indifference, however, is not a deliberate act by most of the universities in these source countries. Saana et al. [69] speculated that high student-faculty ratios result in significant grading loads which need to be completed in a short amount of time. This, together with a lack of plagiarism detection systems at the institution, make it almost impossible to detect plagiarism when it occurs. In addition, the lack of monitoring tools (for example, closed circuit television) makes it difficult for exam invigilators to catch or prevent cheating. Together this leads to plagiarism becoming "accepted practice" in some countries. A student survey conducted in North America across 83 campuses, illustrated that students do not have a clear understanding of what plagiarism is.

A recent news article in BBC News describes a student suing the university for negligence for his plagiarism [70]. According to a student questionnaire survey conducted at the University of Technology, Sydney, Curtin University of Technology, and The University of Sydney [71], international students from Asia face several challenges. They include pedagogy, a teaching methodology different from their home institutions; a preference for fewer student questions and class discussions; a results-based approach rather than a process-based approach; finding class presentations challenging due to a lack of self-confidence, shyness, and self-consciousness of their accent; and language comprehension.

Language difficulties include comprehending textual material, understanding the lectures and taking notes simultaneously, and completing the homework due to a lack of understanding of the requirements. In many cases, significant time is spent looking up words they do not understand.

Cultural differences, adaptation to a new environment, and new policies on aspects of acceptable student practices on issues such as academic dishonesty all contribute to their academic difficulties. This is further complicated by feelings of loneliness, helplessness and homesickness. The value system of students, and socially acceptable behavior norms, may vary between groups of international students, and may differ from that of the local domestic students. For example, some cultures are supportive of each other and do not view some forms of plagiarism as anything other than helping a fellow student; other cultures may not seek help when needed because of a need to save face. In many countries, students are not taught ethical issues surrounding intellectual property and copyright infringement. Students who are not aware of such ethical issues could plagiarize without realizing they are behaving illegally [14, 72].

Unfortunately, cheating is prevalent in some countries. In one example, in 2015, relatives scaled the walls of exam centers to pass cheat sheets to students taking exams [73]. In March 2016, 1,000 candidates took their exam in their underwear to prevent cheating [74]. In another example, to stamp out cheating, authorities blocked mobile internet access when students were taking entrance exams for public sector jobs [75]. There continues to be an industry to help unethical students cheat their way into and through US colleges [76]. In some cultures, plagiarism is viewed as a form of "flattery" since they imitate the original author [22, 72]. A recent article in the Times newspaper in the UK illustrates the alarmingly high rate of plagiarism many universities across the globe face [72]. Faculty may need additional training to better understand the different cultures they are dealing with to avoid branding students from one particular culture as "flagrant plagiarists" [22, 72]. Faculty need to differentiate between deliberate versus unintended plagiarism. Addressing plagiarism in orientation sessions for international students is essential.

4.1. Differences in Pedagogy

International students differ from domestic in the pedagogical demands expected of them during high school or in undergraduate studies. Pedagogy, or teaching practices, differ according to cultural orientation [77, 78]. Individualistic societies tend towards teaching students *how to learn* rather than *how to do things*, and "preparing the individual for a place in society" [78]. On the other hand, in collectivist-oriented societies the emphasis is more on the virtues required to become an effective member of that society [78].

There are several theories regarding cultural integration including, for example, Berry's community based model of cultural integration [79], and Bennett's approach to training for intercultural sensitivity [64]. Alred [80] builds a case understanding intercultural experiences in order to build an appropriate educational response to it. Bender-Szymanski [81] examines mechanisms German teachers use to cope with cultural diversity through cultural conflict. Each model of integration and understanding on intercultural interaction has aspects to commend them, however we adopt the framework of Hofstede [12], and adopted by others [77, 78, 82], and used in several contexts [83, 84], as a mechanism to discuss the challenges. Hofstede's work, while it has its critics (see for example [85]), both provides an understanding of culture *p*er se as well as an insight into cultural difference [86], which in turn provides the insight to analyze challenges faced by international students that relate to cultural difference. Hitchcock et al. [77] and Hofstede et al. [12, 78] point out that collectivist-oriented students have a tendency to hesitate to speak up in larger groups but particularly so when that group contains a number of students outside of that student's culture. The reluctance to speak up decreases in smaller groups. With collectivist-oriented students, the teacher must deal with each student as a part of the group and not isolate them as an individual. Conversely, individualist-oriented students have an expectation that they will be treated as an individual and that they will be treated impartially irrespective of background.

Another cultural orientation issue that affects classroom behavior is power distance. Power distance represents the level of dependence upon a perceived higher authority, such as teachers, as opposed to the levels of interdependence. Cultures with high levels of dependence on authority tend to accept what a higher authority says, as opposed to more consultative or partnership-oriented cultures who more readily approach and contradict their higher authority [77, 78]. High dependence cultures are less likely to question what the teacher puts forward, whereas more interdependent cultures look for a more consultative style with the teacher [77]. Hofstede et al. [78] further point out that in societies with a dependence on higher authority, teaching tends to be teacher-centric. Teachers will outline the paths to be followed, and initiate all the communication, with students speaking only when invited to. Teachers are never publicly contradicted. The knowledge that is transferred is seen as the personal wisdom of the teacher with students remaining dependent on the teacher [78].

In lower power distance societies, however, the teacher and students are seen as equal learning partners. Education tends to be student-centric, with the emphasis on student initiative and finding their own intellectual paths. Students sometimes make uninvited interventions in class, argue with the teacher, express disagreement, even criticisms. The knowledge transferred are facts that exist independently of the teacher [78].

Many orientation sessions for international students do not explain the difference in pedagogy to international students in such a way that they are prepared for the change in classroom culture, expectations and behaviors. Instead, many orientation sessions concentrate on societal differences in general and this often leaves students under-prepared. For faculty and staff guiding students through orientation, it is often difficult to comprehend the magnitude and impact of these cultural changes unless the faculty or staff member has been through the experience themselves.

4.2. External Pressures

As noted above, prior classroom experiences of students may have a significant impact on how well the student integrates into the new environment. Many other external factors impact the student's integration into the classroom, and their level of comfort with their host country's environment.

4.2.1. Time Management

Time can be structured quite differently in some cultures For example, "sequential time" [87] is characterized by scheduling, by doing one task at a time, with only a limited number of events in a given time span with important things being done first and "unimportant" things done last, or not at all if time runs out. On the other hand, "synchronic time" [87] stresses the completion of tasks and maintenance of relationships rather than strict adherence to schedules. In some cultures promptness is not considered to be important. In cyclic time orientation, time is not wasted as could be contended in sequential time orientation [88]. Cyclic time thinkers do things as they naturally occur, or "when it feels right". The time-orientation of the international student, thus, can have a significant effect on the time management required for their study, and on their real or perceived contribution to group-work.

4.2.2. Unconscious Bias (Stereotyping)

While many believe that we are not culturally biased, human beings appear to have a propensity towards one's own culture as the central reality [89, 90].

Unless one's own cultural orientations are understood in relation to other cultural orientations, the result may be unconscious bias by regarding cultural traits as deficits rather than contextual. To avoid unconscious biases, and to cope with cultural diversity, a change in perspective is needed. According to Bender-Szymanski [81], conflict situations between teachers and culturally diverse students must be understood and evaluated in the cultural context of the person being evaluated and not of the evaluator. Hence, academics need to be aware of the cultural orientations that are the basis of international student behaviors.

4.2.3. Societal Networks

To successfully adapt to life in their new community, the international student must build social networks consisting of friends and associates. Social networks play a major role in determining how a person interprets and responds to their environment in a cross-cultural context [91]. Three network types have been identified that are developed by international students: 1) monocultural (among own-culture friends within the host culture), 2) multicultural$_1$ (among own-culture friends plus other foreigners), and 3) multicultural$_2$ (among own culture friends, other foreigners and other local friends) [32, 91, 92].

Movement from a monocultural to a multicultural$_2$ network represents a cross-cultural adjustment away from the student's reliance on home and an increased number and closeness of host culture ties [91]. Many international students, however, tend to remain in a multicultural$_1$ or even the monocultural social network. Thus, adaptation to daily life in their new environment becomes restricted.

4.2.4. Financial Burden

Many students (or their families) take an educational loan to finance their education and have a limited time before the payments begin. Hence, students are under pressure to complete their degree within the shortest time span.

4.2.5. Gender Roles

Students from some cultures have trouble dealing with a female in a position of authority, or even treating females as equals in group assignments. Some cultures differ in having higher expectations from one gender compared to another.

4.2.6. Family Pressures and Expectations

In many cultures, failure not only impacts the individual but the entire extended family. Students are under enormous pressure to do well in school at all costs. Students from collectivist cultures that have the concept of "saving face" have the added pressure of doing well to avoid their family being humiliated [92]. Individualist cultures have no equivalent. The sense of "losing face", therefore, is not readily understood if someone has an individualistic-oriented cultural foundation.

4.2.7. Sense of Identity

Cross-cultural adjustment stress can impact an international student due to loss of familiar cues, a breakdown of interpersonal communication, and identity crisis. Weaver [93] and Shaules [94] argue that international students should seek and respond to adaptation demands rather than remain "sheltered", and have a willingness to accept cultural difference and to allow themselves to change accordingly. When a student overcomes such stresses, genuine psychological growth occurs and the student moves to a deeper level of cultural understanding and adjusts their behaviors [93].

4.2.8. Integration into Daily Life

Adaptation to daily life in another country, and the stresses associated with that, begin immediately upon arrival. For example, the greeting ritual may cause feelings of discomfort, such as invasion of personal space if the greeting involves a higher level of touching than the student is familiar with, or feelings of the host being "cold" if the culture is a "lower-touch" society [35].

The student thus enters the process of cultural adaptation. This process may be short if the perceived cultural distance is close, or may be quite lengthy if the perceived cultural distance is further apart. Perceptions of culture distance arise from differences in cultural values [78, 87]. Cultural distance, experienced by the international student, can have a significant effect on their adaptation to daily life and to their new learning environment. In cases where cultural distance is causing significant adaptation issues, the student may enter a state of culture shock [34].

Students need to understand that education is more than merely completing a set of courses. Students should be "educated" that education is an experience and students get the most out of their education by taking part in local cultural and enrichment activities, learning about other cultures and making friends with students from another culture, and by being part of the community they live in and contributing to it in a positive way.

4.3. Faculty Training

A lack of training for faculty and staff in how to handle cultural issues, and a lack of understanding/appreciation for the challenges of moving to another country may impact how faculty deal with these circumstances. International faculty may have a better understanding of this, however, the possibility of excusing students from one's own country or cultural background while not affording others the same treatment is a risk.

Orientation is set up to help students acclimate but there is little appreciation of the fact that institutions essentially ask students to abandon their value system and attitudes toward issues such as plagiarism (which they may perceive as simply helping each other), and adopt the value system of the host country immediately in order to be successful.

5. Orientation Practices

Some of the challenges faced by international students include navigating the educational system, culture shock, time management, language and cultural issues. The support provided by institutions alleviates these issues to some extent. Students are also informed about the various enrichment activities available (speaker series, film nights, various campus clubs, athletic facilities, discounts available to students) on- and off-campus and are encouraged to take part in some of these activities so they get the most out of their academic life. The on-campus orientation sessions are aimed at mitigating these challenges and facilitating the students transition to the host country so that they can enjoy their time there.

To help address the challenges international students face, most institutions, and all institutions represented in the study, have orientation programs of varied lengths and formats. Their key focus is an attempt to integrate students into the institutional culture, and to improve their chance of successfully progressing through, and completing, their degree program. Not all programs offer an orientation program or segment specifically aimed at the needs of international students. This section focuses on the orientation programs of each author's institution. Common elements are covered first and any unique or note-worthy characteristics of an individual institution are highlighted.

Each focus institution offers an orientation program prior to the start of the student's first semester, with a full range of academic and cultural assimilation programs, while a few have additional follow-up programs that run at various times through the first semester. Each institution allocates a staff or student adviser to a small group of students. In each institution, several areas of the university are involved in delivering the orientation program. Faculty expressed concern that each area was focused on their own area of responsibility, with little thought to the overall message as experienced by the student. Further, most teaching staff are not aware of the detail covered in orientation programs, which sometimes leads to students receiving contradictory messages.

A strong faculty perception is that while orientation programs are generally successful, students still struggle with a range of challenges which hinder the successful transition to the host institution. While both domestic and international students struggle with the move from high school to a university environment, international students face additional significant cultural and academic changes both at the start and during the program.

Orientation programs attempting to address these challenges are often in the week or two prior to the start of semester. This coincides with the time period when international students are experiencing significant culture shock, since international students typically arrive in the host country immediately prior to the orientation program. In this period of confusion, attempts are made to introduce students to the host culture and describe and explain numerous academic strategies and policies. The sheer volume of material being disseminated in this intense period can add to the sense of confusion and chaos.

With the dissemination of information, little thought is given to the variance in the international student population. A review of the orientation programs of the institutions in this study show that international students are generally treated as a homogeneous group, while the reality is that even students from the same country have significant differences in the population (for example, the north and south of India). Some institutions are in the position where all students in the program are international students, making it difficult to provide cultural assimilation via osmosis.

While each of the focus institutions have mandatory orientation programs, many students miss these sessions, due to visa issues, etc. In most instances, these students receive less or no orientation and are often less successful than their counterparts who had attended the full orientation program. In addition, their first experience of a "mandatory" program in the host country is that its meaning is flexible, possibly leading to the interpretation that there is flexibility in all policies.

A small number of institutions, typically the institutions with larger international populations and often those with an international campus, hold pre-arrival orientation sessions. These typically provide advice to students on what they can expect on arrival and what documentation is required to do things such as open a bank account. These pre-arrival orientation sessions are not a replacement for the on-campus orientation program, but are typically an attempt to reduce the initial culture shock and feeling of being overwhelmed that many students face.

Most institutions identified improving the quality of the orientation program as a major challenge, in terms of information retention and the value it offers the students when the time available for the orientation is limited.

5.1. On-Campus Orientation

While some institutions offer a pre-arrival orientation, all focus institutions provide an orientation program on arrival for international students. This on-campus orientation session is typically held immediately prior to the start of the semester, but in some instances, orientation activities continue into the first semester of study.

The typical on-campus orientation covers university practices and policies, academic integrity, time management, housing, how to open a bank account, advice for academic success (study skills), and activities/events to help with integration into the institutional community. On-campus orientation can vary in length from one day to one week, for example Northwest Missouri State University and Valley View University hold a week-long orientation program for new students. The orientation provided to undergraduate and graduate international students differs at some institutions, and may extend beyond the week prior to the start of class. For example Northwest Missouri State University, undergraduate students (international and domestic) are required to take a course named University Seminar that discusses academic integrity, how to use proper citations [95], study skills, and other skills to increase their chance of success in their academic program. This course takes place in their first semester after they have completed the orientation session prior to the start of the semester. Other institutions explicitly compress this content into the orientation session prior to the start of the semester.

Some institutions, for example Mount Royal University, have both domestic and international students attend orientation together. Although issues maybe similar for both cohorts, there are many matters that concern just the international students. These matters are not specifically addressed. Other institutions hold separate orientations however do not address cultural difference matters specifically.

In the main, the content covered in the orientation sessions for international students is similar to that for domestic students albeit with an enhanced focus on language, the culture of the host institution and host country, and advice on navigating society and life such as opening bank accounts and where to find ingredients for cooking. Some institutions have recognized that the orientation sessions are not as successful as they would like. Some institutions hold orientation sessions and then simply assign a faculty advisor or mentor to students to provide guidance throughout the year. For example, Northwest Missouri State University assigns 2-3 international students to interested faculty through its Friends of International Students program. The faculty and students interact frequently throughout the academic year. Students are often invited to attend Thanksgiving dinner with the faculty member and their family, or go on sight seeing trips together.

Some institutions have a unique situation or mission and find that their orientation sessions are successful. Orientation at Berea College begins with an on-line pre-arrival orientation followed by four live-stream orientation meetings over the summer. These are followed by a week-long on-campus orientation immediately before classes begin which includes social, cultural, and academic activities covering many aspects of life at Berea College from banking to academic honesty. Berea College uses a cohort model for academic advising in which the students' first term writing instructor also serves as the academic advisor with 16 students per advisor. Each first-term writing course also has an upper-level student who serves as a peer leader. During the week-long orientation students meet and spend time with their academic advisor and peer leader.

5.2. Pastoral Care and Support Services

All focus group institutions have broadly similar headline support for students. As part of orientation students are introduced to the range of support services available to them throughout their time at university. These typically include:

- Peer mentors
- Facebook groups
- Support staff
- Course directors
- Weekly newsletters
- Central support services

All new students are allocated an academic advisor for the duration of their studies, whom they meet as part of the orientation process. Thereafter students are offered regular meetings throughout the course of their degree program, some to specifically help choose courses (typically a mandatory meeting) and other meetings just to monitor progress and ensure well-being (typically optional). Optional meetings are typically poorly attended. The advisor is also there as a point of contact for any issues that may arise during the period of a student's registration; the advisor is expected to provide academic guidance and some level of personal support to help students assimilate into the local community. The mission is to create a relationship of shared responsibility between academic advisors and students that supports the development and implementation of educational plans that align with students' goals.

Services are also offered to help with academic work, such as report writing and referencing, but these are mainly services that students must proactively seek, although on occasion they may be referred for help. Many institutions monitor student attendance at class and if a student is not attending on a regular and frequent basis, an alert is sent to the student's advisor for follow-up and intervention as appropriate. Students who fail to attend class risk having their registration terminated and this has severe consequences in terms of their visa status.

Most institutions have student groups such as the Indian Students Association. which allows students to converse in their native tongue, share regional food, and provide advice regarding the local community such as where to purchase ingredients for cooking.

All students, domestic and international, with a disability (including learning disabilities) are encouraged to register with the student support and wellbeing team to obtain extra help and support tailored to their needs, be this mentoring, extra time in examinations, or a note taker.

5.3. Academic Support

5.3.1. Academic Integrity Policies and Communication

At each of the focus group institutions, students are first informed of policies on academic integrity during their initial orientation sessions. All of the focus institutions also include a statement on academic integrity on the course outline or course syllabus. Some institutions, such as Valley View University, explicitly identify falsification of official documents as academic dishonesty even though it may occur prior to the student even enrolling at the institution.

The following are some other ways the focus institutions inform students about academic integrity policies. Note that these are not all unique to international students:

- The undergraduate students at the University of Kent have a compulsory first stage to their degree program and one of the first semester modules includes plagiarism, citations, group work and report writing. This provides an introduction to the topic and explains how the student is expected to conduct themselves in the host culture; indeed, the first assessment is about plagiarism and how to avoid it.

- A question/answer session to gather the students' perspective on what constitutes plagiarism in their opinion. Unfortunately, often the students will answer with what they think the instructor wants to hear, rather than provide their own point of view.
- Most instructors inform or discuss academic dishonesty, usually through talks, videos, etc., before assigning their first assignment.
- Copies of the academic integrity policies are made available in the school or departmental office and also posted on the school's web site.
- A copy of the policy, together with a written statement of the instructor's specific rules on cooperation and use of published sources, is distributed to all students in the course.
- For each assignment students are reminded about the expectations for academic integrity and, in some cases, must sign or acknowledge that they have abided by these expectations.

Despite the frequency and consistency with which students hear warnings on academic integrity, violations still occur. As has been mentioned, the reasons for engaging in academic dishonesty are varied, with some of the rationale being cultural (for example, this is accepted practice in the home country), based on external factors (for example, financial pressure does not allow for a student to do poorly in a class), or inconsistency on behalf of faculty (for example, previous behavior went unpunished). When the frequency with which students are reminded of their expected behavior is high, students may simply stop listening.

The process for charging a student with academic dishonesty include documenting the accusation and circumstances of the action undertaken by the student that is regarded by the faculty member as academic dishonesty. A typical process permits the student to appeal to a committee formed within the school, and if that appeal is unsuccessful, they have the right to appeal to an institutional panel. The level of documentation and time required to charge a student is regarded by some faculty as burdensome. As a result, some instances of academic dishonesty are handled by the faculty member without utilizing the documented process.

In cases when academic dishonesty is reported, violations are typically heard by a school-wide or university-wide committee and records of those found guilty of violations are stored in the student's file. Then for second, or subsequent offenses, penalties become more severe, up to and including expulsion from the program or institution.

5.3.2. Academic Integrity Challenges for International Students

It is well acknowledged that academic integrity is an essential component of higher education. Education is both the acquisition of knowledge and the development of skills that lead to further intellectual development, As such, faculty are expected to follow strict principles of intellectual honesty in their own scholarship; students are held to the same standard. Only by doing their own work can students gain the knowledge, skills, confidence and self-worth that come from earned success; only by learning how to gather information, to integrate it and to communicate it effectively, to identify an idea and follow it to its logical conclusion can they develop the habits of mind characteristic of educated citizens. Taking shortcuts to secure higher grades, or an easier pathway, results in an educational experience that is intellectually bankrupt.

Although all of the focus institutions publish and communicate institutional, departmental, and course-level academic integrity policies (see as examples [96, 97], all of the members of the authors' focus group identified plagiarism as a prevalent problem. Most institutions, such as the Auckland University of Technology, place the academic integrity policy in every course through its on-line learning management system. Some institutions discuss plagiarism prior to the first assignment in each course, others such as the University of Kent, also place the policy on the cover sheet of every assessment instrument. However, plagiarism remains an issue.

However, the focus group reports very different experiences in their respective focus institutions. Each institution's document describing academic integrity policies also defined what constitutes academic dishonesty, providing explicit examples in many cases, and describing the process for dealing with plagiarism once it was detected. Each of the focus institutions screens for plagiarism using tools such as Turnitin which in many cases is embedded within the learning management system used on that campus. International students are typically reminded that if they are unsure if something would constitute academic dishonesty, they can talk to their instructor or advisor to seek clarification. Some institutions (for example, Eastern Institute of Technology) offer help in the areas in which students may be struggling. This could be academic writing, paraphrasing, report writing or others depending on the issues. These sessions are held at lunchtime (to avoid clashes with classes) once or twice a week for any student to attend.

Some institutions (for example, Northwest Missouri State University) requires students to complete a short quiz at the beginning of each course before the content of that course is unlocked in the learning management system. This requires the students to attest that they have read and understand the policy on academic integrity, understand the consequences for engaging in academic dishonesty, and a pledge that they will not practice academic dishonesty in that course. This is necessary because faculty and school recommendations on plagiarism cases have been overturned on student appeal at the university level because they felt the school had not been explicit enough about defining plagiarism and its consequences. This committee consists primarily of faculty from the Arts and Humanities and they typically have little understanding of coding and what plagiarism in code looks like. Furthermore, this committee has insisted on levels of proof of academic dishonesty that are onerous or impossible to prove. Even in cases when a faculty member has observed two students talking to each other during an exam, there are examples where the charge of academic dishonesty has been overturned due to a lack of evidence to refute the student's denial of the event.

For those students pursuing a computing degree, international students are charged with academic dishonesty at a higher rate than domestic students at some, but not all, of the focus institutions. Many international students may subjectively interpret the academic integrity based on their cultural understanding. Examples of academic dishonesty that have been detected at the focus institutions include copying work not authored by the student, passing answers (written or oral) during an exam, use of cell phones and smart watches during exams [98], collusion, buying solutions to an assessment, and submitting answers from a student who recently completed the course. In addition, plagiarism of software assignments most likely occurs but is much more difficult to prove due to the lack of maturity of plagiarism detection tools focused on code.

Members of the focus group identified several challenges that international students face in adhering to academic integrity expectations in the focus institution. Many international students may have an inadequate understanding of what constitutes plagiarism and some lack the skills and training to avoid plagiarism [99]. As mentioned earlier, there are cultural differences regarding what constitutes helping others, and the fine line between helping and plagiarizing interpreted differently between the students and the faculty member. Some focus institutions offer question/answer sessions on what constitutes plagiarism in the student's opinion, these faculty report that international students do not perceive many things as academically dishonest that instructors and domestic students consider plagiarism. This is perhaps due to cultural expectations.

The sense among the focus group is that their institutions communicate the academic integrity policy and expectations clearly and that the students understand the policy. At several of the focus institutions those students charged with academic dishonesty, and who admit to the activity, typically say that they were aware that what they were doing was inappropriate and constituted academic dishonesty. Those students who do not admit to the charge typically deny that they engaged in the activity rather than argue that the activity itself was not an instance of academic dishonesty. This suggests that students are aware of what they are doing but engage in academically dishonest practices for other reasons, such as external pressure, and the relatively low rate of detection and conviction. Students also face different staff interpretations of policy that leads to confusion and misunderstanding. It is also likely that the sheer volume of discussion on academic integrity (during orientation, at the beginning of every course, posted on each course web site, printed at the beginning of every assessment instrument) is counterproductive in itself, as students simply learn to ignore it rather than recognize it as something of importance.

5.4. Mentoring and Financial Support

Most of the focus institutions provide mentoring for all students, domestic and international, by ensuring that every student is assigned an academic advisor. Some institutions also assign a peer mentor to international students to provide support from a peer as opposed to someone perceived to be an authority figure. Peer mentoring works well at some institutions but is less successful at others as the peer mentors have their own classes to attend and assignments to complete. This was the case at Valley View University where the faculty tried several mentoring programs with failed results. One of the models used assigned freshmen and sophomore students a peer mentor who was a senior student. This program failed because the seniors were too busy with their own projects to give their mentees sufficient time. Furthermore, there was no proper monitoring from the faculty.

Peer mentors, or paid teaching assistants typically provide "help sessions" or organize study groups to provide academic support. The teaching assistants are typically trained in some way, and are provided support from the course instructor. When the international student fills the role of teaching assistant they are put in a position to deliver content in the style appropriate to the host culture and this helps that individual to assimilate more fully, and better appreciate the academic environment, especially when the program of study is not made up entirely of one ethnic group. Attending help sessions also provides international students with an opportunity to socialize and integrate into the university community as help sessions are open to all students and not restricted to international students,

International students are often perceived as revenue streams by the administration. International students typically pay tuition often at a much higher rate than domestic or in-state students, and are often ineligible for scholarship support. Many institutions offer tuition discounting in order to attract and retain high quality students; for example, a student maintaining an A grade average may receive a tuition discount of 25%. Often the only source of income for international students is a part-time job on campus. Many departments offer employment as a graduate teaching assistant, or research assistant. These jobs typically help defray the living expenses the student faces. However, the pressure to secure a scholarship or a teaching assistantship may contribute to the pressure on a student to engage in academically dishonest practices. Furthermore, the faculty are one step removed from grading and hence detection of academic dishonesty becomes more difficult as the faculty are reliant on cases being reported by the teaching assistant. At some institutions, there have been instances of the teaching assistant granting access to the gradebook to fellow students by password sharing, or the teaching assistant changing the grade of a fellow student after pressure is applied to them by another student. The situation is often worse when the teaching assistant is taking the class themselves as sometimes happens at smaller institutions.

Berea College is unique in that it charges no tuition fee and all students work for the College. Hence, all computer science courses have one or more teaching assistants and international students do not face the same financial stresses as at other institutions.

5.5. Faculty Perceptions

Faculty members who are involved in orientation sessions have an awareness of the content of the orientation topics covered. However, many faculty are not involved in delivering the orientation material and may not be aware of the topics addressed. These faculty tend to make assumptions about the student's background and experience that may be inaccurate. In addition, for example, if a class, A, from an undergraduate program is identified as requiring prerequisite knowledge for a graduate class, B, then it is possible that the academic coordinator awards an international student credit for class A based on the student having completed a class similar to A at their previous institution. However, it is possible that an instructor teaching course B assumes specific knowledge from A which may not be known to the student. Many faculty teaching classes assume that the students in the class have a homogeneous background which perfectly matches the course taught at the current institution. For many faculty, this extends further in assuming that all students have experience with the educational system used at the current institution and that all students have similar attitudes towards academic integrity etc.

When a case of academic dishonesty is detected, the paperwork to be completed and level of proof discourages some faculty from following the university process. Some faculty implement a penalty without recording the fact that students engaged in academically dishonest activities. This unfortunately sends a message to the student body that academic dishonesty is not treated seriously and that a student should claim it is their first offense if they are ever caught.

6. Survey Results

A survey was conducted of students studying at several of the focus institutions in the US (3 institutions), UK (1 institution), New Zealand (2 institutions) and Ghana (1 institution). The survey consisted of several parts, each designed to gather information on aspects of the students international education experience. The survey is exploratory in nature and was set up to gain a better understanding the students point of view in order to build a more targeted survey at a later time. The survey aimed to find out if there was any significant differences or similarities in responses based on the host country or the source country. The survey results should also be able to lend credence, or otherwise, to widely held faculty perceptions and hence inform a more thorough investigation at a later date. The structure of the survey consists of six parts as follows:

1. Questions soliciting non-identifying personal information.

2. Questions relating to the host country's orientation program.

3. Statements, against which students identify their level of agreement (select one of strongly disagree, disagree, neutral, agree, strongly agree, N/A), about the success of the orientation program in terms of preparing the students for a new culture and academic environment.

4. Statements, against which students identify their level of agreement, about the courses they are studying and their personal study habits.

5. Statements, against which students identify their level of agreement, about the degree program that the student is studying toward.

6. A small set of open-ended questions.

Each of these parts is examined in turn below. Students could not choose multiple items from a list of options and were thus forced to select the most appropriate response.

All international students that were in computer science programs at the selected focus institutions were invited to participate in the survey. Participation was completely voluntary and no personal identifying information was gathered. Students were free to choose to not answer some questions while choosing to answer others. All international students at the selected focus institutions were E-mailed a link to the the survey and asked if they would participate. Every attempt was made to get the broadest coverage possible, but the non-alignment of academic calendars in the Northern and Southern hemisphere meant that some students were nearing the end of a semester when the survey was administered. The survey was pretested by using a small number of international faculty who were previously international students, or have extensive experience with international students, to provide experimental answers and an expert opinion. This survey itself is considered exploratory and the results obtained will guide its refinement and evolution in order to gather more specific data.

The first part of the survey consisted of seven questions and collected basic personal and demographic information. The survey attracted 210 responses from international students. Part 1 of the survey revealed that the students were studying in the USA (76.08%), New Zealand (19.62%), Ghana (2.87%), and the UK (1.44%). The source countries for the students include: Albania, Bulgaria, Bangladesh, Bolivia, China, Dominican Republic, Eritrea, Estonia, Equatorial Guinea, Ethiopia, Ghana, Haiti, India, Italy, Jordan, Kenya, Kosovo, Korea, Kyrgyzstan, Macedonia, Mauritius, Malaysia, Mongolia, Montenegro, Nepal, Nigeria, Philippines, Somalia, Sierra Leone, Sri Lanka, South Sudan, Tajikistan, Thailand, Vietnam, Zambia, and Zimbabwe. India, with 140 responses (84.85%), represented the largest source country. China was the next largest with 10 responses (6.06%), followed by Nigeria with six responses (3.64%), and Nepal with five responses (3.03%). All other countries contributed only one to two responses. A total of 47 students declined to answer this question. The large number of Indian students is a reflection of the international student populations in the focus institutions. For example, Northwest Missouri State University's graduate program consists of approximately 98% Indian students mostly coming from a single city within India (Hyderabad). Similarly the Eastern Institute of Technology in New Zealand has a graduate program consisting of over 80% Indian students and the remainder are primarily Chinese.

The disproportionate number of responses from Indian students had the potential to skew the results, yet there were not sufficient numbers of students from the other source countries in order to identify marked differences between cohorts from any two countries. However when all non-Indian student responses are aggregated and compared to the Indian student cohort, there are no notable discrepancies in the results. Consequently, the survey illustrates that international students face similar challenges adjusting to the new culture and expectations of the host country independent of where they chose to study or what their original source country is. This is, perhaps, unsurprising since the survey does not focus on the student's cultural identity, but rather focuses on how well the host institution is doing to assimilate the international student into the local culture and education system. For the purposes of examining how well institutions perform in guiding and helping students with the challenges they face, the group of international students surveyed can be treated as a homogeneous group. However, when considering the specific challenges students from one country face compared to another country, it is most likely that the students can not be treated as homogeneous.

Data was not collected on the institution the student previously studied at, or at which institution they are currently completing their international education. Data was only gathered at the country level. Of the respondents, 161 students (76.3%) indicated that they chose to study in the US, 41 students (19.43%) identified New Zealand as their host country, six students (2.84%) identify Ghana, and three students (1.42%) identified the UK. One student declined to provide the information. Comparison of the results for the largest two destination countries revealed no notable discrepancies in the data. This, again, was unsurprising given that each of the four host countries attempt to orient and integrate the students in a similar fashion.

Students elected to pursue international education primarily because they believed that:

- the host country's educational system was superior (82 students, 39.04%),
- there was a perception of availability of better opportunities, (72 students, 33.96%),
- they intended to seek employment in the host country on graduation (26 students, 12.26%),
- the host institution offered courses that matched their interest (19 students, 8.96%), or
- they explicitly wanted to gain exposure to the host countries culture (10 students, 4.71%).

A total of eight students (3.77%) identified other reasons including cost, Berea College's free tuition and work study program, attracted to a specific college, passion for the USA (specific country), admission practices, and to gain international exposure and understand aspects of business culture. Three students declined to provide a reason for choosing their host country and institution.

The low percentage of students identifying a strong interest in learning the culture of the host country may contribute to the observation made on many campuses that international students have a tendency to primarily socialize with students from the same country. The relatively low interests in the host country's culture may also translate to a lack of desire to modify behavior to match the local culture and attitudes.

Of the 212 survey respondents, 1.57% are pursuing a doctoral qualification, 70.16% of students are pursuing a Master's degree, 26.18% are pursuing a Bachelor's degree, and the remainder are seeking an Associate's degree. 84.62% of the respondents are seeking a degree in Computer Science, 13.74% in Information Technology, 1.10% in Information Systems, and 0.55% in Software Engineering. Respondents were approximately equally distributed across the first four semesters of the program of study and a small number (11.79%) were beyond the fourth semester.

The second part of the survey consisted of four questions asking if the host institution provided some kind of training or orientation covering of the differences between the source country and the host country, both in terms of culture as well as academic structure and expectations, and whether the student felt this introduction was adequate. Coverage of local culture was not a part of every host institution's orientation program. When asked if the student felt that the host institution provided training, mentoring, or held discussions to help them acclimate to the host country's culture, 167 students (84.50%) agreed, while 31 students (15.5%) disagreed. When asked if they felt that this coverage is adequate, 137 students (69.90%) felt it was, 42 students (21.43%) felt it was inadequate, and 17 students (8.67%) felt the question was not applicable.

When asked if the host institution provided training, mentoring, or discussions on academic issues such as plagiarism, the need to observe deadlines, and potential differences in grading scales, 176 (89.34%) agreed that the topics were covered while 21 students (10.66%) felt it was not addressed. When asked if they felt that the coverage of these topics was adequate, 160 students (80.81%) felt it was adequate, and 31 students (15.66%) felt it was inadequate. Seven students (3.54%) felt the question was not applicable. Despite the fact that only 89.34% thought that this was covered in the orientation delivered by the host institution, each of the host institutions confirmed that these topics had been covered during orientation. Only 80.81% found that the discussion of academic integrity during orientation was adequate.

A total of 160 of 210 (76.19%) of respondents thought that the host institution coverage of plagiarism and academic integrity was adequate. Of the students who felt it was inadequate, just under half felt that the host institution provided no orientation in plagiarism and academic integrity, while just over half indicated that the institution did cover plagiarism and academic integrity during orientation. This is in contrast to the perceptions of faculty that the issues surrounding academic integrity are covered multiple times throughout orientation and at the beginning of each course. Of the 5.08% of students who admitted to engaging in plagiarism, 80% felt that plagiarism and academic integrity was adequately covered in the orientation. One can conclude that they knowingly engaged in plagiarism because of some perceived benefit or external pressure, but the likelihood is that they have not yet been caught.

Table 1, the third part of the survey, provides insight into the student's perception of how well they integrated into the host country's culture and academic environment. Results for students who identified a question as "not applicable" are omitted from the table and hence each row does not necessarily sum to 100%. Table 1 shows that 82.45% of students believed (agree or strongly agree) that they were adapting to the culture of their host country and that they were enjoying and appreciating the experience. Their experience in the host country had made >80% more culturally aware than they were prior to leaving their home country. Arguably, the international experience is having a positive impact on creating well-rounded and culturally aware individuals.

The 4th part of the survey examined the students perceptions of the courses they were undertaking and any challenges associated with those courses, and their study habits, When examining the academic environment more closely, only 73.10% reported that they were not experiencing any significant language barriers. However, 81.85% of the respondent's reported that they were not experiencing communication barriers when writing. Consequently, presentations and speaking within a group setting may cause stress to some international students. In each case, more than 80% of the respondents reported understanding the grading scheme (86.17%), expectations of quality of work (89.31%), and policies regarding late submission of assignments (93.05%). 86.71% of the students responded positively to adapting to the change in academic environment from their home country. This suggests that the orientation into the host coun-

Table 1. Integration into a new culture and academic environment

To what extent do you agree with each statement: Statement	Strongly Disagree	Disagree	Neutral	Agree	Strongly Agree
I am adapting to the cultural differences between my home and host country:	2.13	3.7	11.17	44.68	37.77
I am enjoying and appreciating the cultural differences between my home and host country.	1.60	1.60	11.23	43.32	41.18
I am more culturally aware, and appreciate and celebrate the differences, than I was prior to studying in my host country.	1.60	2.13	13.39	42.55	38.83
I am not experiencing any language barriers when I speak to people.	4.26	6.38	14.89	34.57	38.83
I am not experiencing any communication barriers when I communicate in writing (reports, essays, manuals, etc).	1.60	4.79	11.70	38.83	43.02
I have adapted to the differences in academic standards and experiences between my home and host countries.	1.60	1.06	9.57	43.62	43.09
I understand and have adapted to the grading scheme used in my host country.	1.06	1.06	10.11	41.49	44.68
I understand the host country's definition of plagiarism.	1.62	0.54	3.24	40.54	53.51
I understand the host institution's policy regarding late submission of assignments.	1.07	2.14	3.21	39.04	54.01
I understand the host institution's expectations regarding quality and depth of work when writing essays and answering assignments.	1.60	0.53	8.02	43.32	45.99

try's culture and the academic environment is having a positive impact.

Table 2 looks a little more deeply into the student's perception of course content and their study skills. 87.01% of students feel that they participate in class discussion. In addition, 88.63% believe that they are learning valuable soft skills including presentations and conflict resolution. This would imply that even though some may feel uncomfortable with their language skills, there is general appreciation for the fact that they are asked to deliver class presentations and engage in group work.

Approximately 5% of the students indicated that they plagiarize (5.08%), act unethically (5.08%) and unprofessionally (3.95%) (responses of strongly disagree, disagree, or neutral). This indicates that at least 5% of the students knowingly and deliberately engaged in academic dishonesty. Some seemingly believe it is possible to behave unethically or plagiarize, yet still behave professionally. Another interpretation of the data is that some students may not invest time in thinking about, or attempting to solve, a problem prior to seeking assistance.

Table 2. Perceptions of course content and study skills

To what extent do you agree with each statement: Statement	Strongly Disagree	Disagree	Neutral	Agree	Strongly Agree
I participate in class discussions.	1.13	3.39	8.47	39.55	47.46
I am learning valuable soft skills (listening, presenting, communicating, conflict resolution, etc).	2.27	1.70	7.39	43.18	45.45
I do not engage in plagiarism.	1.13	0.00	3.95	32.20	62.71
I always behave in an ethical manner.	1.13	0.00	3.95	32.20	62.71
I always behave in a professional manner.	1.13	0.56	2.26	35.03	61.02
I always seek help as soon as I am having difficulties with class materials.	1.69	7.91	15.25	38.42	36.16
I usually seek help from a friend rather than the class instructor.	4.52	14.69	27.68	25.42	27.12
I use the internet as my main source of help.	1.13	2.82	14.12	36.16	45.29
I buy and read the textbook.	10.23	17.61	26.14	23.86	20.45
I leave assignments until the last minute.	18.18	32.39	24.43	11.36	12.50

23.86% of students indicated that they left their assignments until the last minute, and 74.58% indicated that they sought help as soon as they encountered difficulties in an assignment. Generally, these are encouraging numbers as it shows students proactively seeking to address areas of misunderstanding as early as possible (albeit late in some instances from the faculty member's perspective).

Examining where students seek assistance, Table 2 shows that 52.54% seek help from their friends as a primary source. While students are often encouraged by faculty to use each other as a resource, if students do not fully understand and reject plagiarism, this has the potential to be problematic. 81.45% of students indicated that the internet was their primary source of information and only 44.31% of the respondents indicated that they buy and read the textbook. While the internet is a valuable resource, cutting and pasting content is readily detected in essays with tools such as Turnitin. However, plagiarized code is still more difficult to detect and prove.

The 5th part of the survey examines the student's perceptions of their program of study in general (Table 3). 76.51% of students believe that instructors grade fairly and consistently and only 70.49% believe that they are treated equally to their local peers. Seeking extra time to complete assignments was regarded as acceptable to 49.39% of respondents and 36.75% believed it was acceptable to ask for extra points or marks in an assignment. This may demonstrate a cultural difference between domestic and international students in general.

Even though the orientation and assimilation practices of most institutions include assigning international students a faculty advisor, only 69.88% believe that they are provided sound advice. Only 69.69% of students believe that they are awarded the grade that they deserve in a class with 35.54% claiming that the work was too difficult, and 37.55% claiming that the hands-on approach to learning was a challenge. Notably, most students did not believe that they were being asked to do too much work. Perceptions that the work is difficult and challenges with the hands-on teaching pedagogy provide additional pressure to engage in academic dishonesty.

54.27% of the respondents reported that their social interactions were mostly with others from their home country. 40.50% stated that they use their mother tongue when speaking to other students from their country on campus. While this is most likely because it is the most comfortable language for them to use, 50.83% indicated that they intended to stay in the host country and seek employment on graduation. Hence this is a lost opportunity to refine their language and communication skills which Table 1 illustrated was a challenge for approximately 35% of the students.

The final part of the survey provided students to answer six open-ended questions. Results are presented in Tables 4-9. All answers were reviewed and key themes identified. These were used to group results for reporting purposes. Noteworthy comments were identified as those that summarized a key point made by respondents, or provided an insight that stood out, or offered a unique perspective.

Examining the open feedback and grouping comments together, some interesting observations can be made. Table 4 shows that 17% of the written responses indicated that there was no similarity between the educational systems of the home and host countries, while 43.5% indicated some strong similarities of which 8.5% claimed everything was similar. One noteworthy comment expressed disappointment in the amount of rote learning required in a Master's degree in the US as the student was expecting to be forced to think and be more creative.

Table 3. Perceptions of the program of study in general

To what extent do you agree with each statement: Statement	Strongly Disagree	Disagree	Neutral	Agree	Strongly Agree
I believe instructors in the host country grade fairly and consistently.	3.01	6.02	13.25	44.58	31.93
I believe I am treated equally to local students.	6.63	6.02	13.25	31.33	39.16
I think it is acceptable to ask for extra time to complete an assignment.	9.64	17.47	22.29	30.72	18.67
I think it is acceptable to ask for extra points/marks in an assignment.	13.25	22.89	25.30	20.48	16.27
I get good feedback from instructors that helps me improve.	3.01	3.61	11.45	47.59	33.13
Faculty provide sound advice on how I approach my work/study.	5.42	3.61	19.88	40.36	29.52
Generally, I receive the grade I believe I deserve in each course.	6.06	4.85	18.18	39.39	30.30
I find the work too difficult in the courses I take.	9.04	22.29	31.93	22.29	13.25
I think I am asked to do too much work in each class.	6.799	27.78	34.57	15.43	13.38
There is more flexibility in courses in my host country than in my home country.	6.63	9.04	24.10	34.34	24.10
There is more structure in courses in my host country than in my home country.	4.91	11.04	25.77	35.58	20.66
I feel challenged by the courses I am taking.	3.05	9.15	17.68	43.29	25.61
I find the hands-on approach to teaching in the host country to be difficult.	5.45	24.85	29.09	23.03	14.55
My social interactions are mostly with people from my home country.	7.88	17.58	18.79	31.82	22.45
When on campus, I speak to students from my home country in my native language.	12.27	26.38	19.63	20.25	20.25
I plan on staying in the host country after graduation.	7.27	9.70	28.48	25.45	24.85

Table 4. What are the greatest similarities between the educational system in your home country and your host country?

Category	Count	%	Remark
What are the greatest similarities between the educational system in your home country and your host country?	16	17.0	No similarity
	12	12.7	Educational expectations
	11	11.7	Syllabus
	10	10.6	Exams
	8	8.5	Everything is similar

Noteworthy comments:

I believe we have similar grading system, with assignments, labs with hands on practice at the masters level courses. Also the rote learning stuff is quite rampant in the masters level. I thought initially this would be eliminated here in US and we would be forced to think and be creative.

Table 5. What are the greatest differences between the educational system in your home country and your host country?

Category	Count	%	Remark
What are the greatest differences between the educational system in your home country and your host country?	21	23.7	Assessment and grading scheme
	21	23.7	Practical approach
	18	20.3	Education system
	14	15.8	Teaching method
	8	9.0	Curriculum

Noteworthy comments:

The greatest differences are the availability of the instructors to help (their office hours are very flexible) and the many opportunities available to accompany us in our study.

The courses that I take in the host country go well in depth and I have way more assignments compared to my home country. I am offered opportunities such as internships and hands on experience while undertaking the classes, something my country doesn't do. There is a lot more group work involved in the computer science classes as opposed to working on by myself as I would have in my country. The resources such as office hours and computer science lab to help students are two great things that I take advantage of when bettering myself. My home country lacks resources. In other word, my home country does not provide a laptop for every student so everything is taught in theory rather than students working on problems on their own. In the classes in my host country I am given homework throughout the semester whereas in my home country my grade is dependent on one single exam. The professors at my host university are more qualified than my home country.

It is more cut-throat in my home country than in the host country. Classes in the host country are more practical and supported by resources/materials/labs necessary to successfully learn the subject. Education in the host country is more hands-on.

Teachers were more helpful and provided with part time job references. The teachers in my home country were leading professionals in the Industry and they were not racists.

In my home country we must select our major right at the start of the bachelor's degree. If at some point along the way we decide to change it, we must start over. In my host country, usually one can decide on a major after a good amount of time to be able to make a sound decision (in liberal arts at least).

Table 5 examines comments relating to the greatest differences in the educational systems of the home and host countries. Responses identified the greatest differences to be assessment and grading, the practical hands-on approach utilized, the educational system in general, teaching methods and the curriculum. The noteworthy comments highlighted the high availability and flexibility of the faculty in the host country and the appropriate infrastructure provided to support the hands-on teaching approach.

Turning to the similarities in culture between the host and home countries in Table 6, 35.9% of the written responses identified friendliness and respect as similarities, but 12.6% indicated that there were no similarities.

Examining the greatest differences between the home and host countries reveals some interesting responses. Table 7 highlights that 26.5% of written responses identified differences in cultural norms and values as the greatest difference, 12.2% identified social interactions and communication as substantially different with an additional 3.1% specifically identifying non-verbal communi-

Table 6. What is the greatest similarity between the culture in your home country and the host country?

Category	Count	%	Remark
What is the greatest similarity between the culture in your home country and the host country?	25	24.3	Friendly and helpful
	13	12.6	No similarity
	12	11.6	Respect
	5	4.9	Not much different
	3	2.9	Parties and celebrations

Table 7. What is the greatest differences between the culture in your home country and the host country?

Category	Count	%	Remark
What is the greatest differences between the culture in your home country and the host country?	26	26.5	Responses related to cultural norms and values
	12	12.2	Social interactions and communication
	7	7.1	Food
	5	5.1	The culture
	3	3.1	Non-verbal communication
	3	3.1	Not much similarity
	3	3.1	Racism

cation. A total of 3.1% of the respondents identified racism in the host country as a difference. This table identifies the primary shortcomings of the cultural introduction to the host country delivered as part of the orientation program.

Table 8 shows responses when students were asked what they missed from their home country. 63.3% of the responses identified food in their response with 32.2% solely identifying food in their response. 62.2% of the respondents identified parents/family as what they missed the most. 35.5% identified the environment, social activities, and tradition as something that they missed. The cultural ties and the bond to family and friends is strong. It is unrealistic to expect that students can adapt to the host countries culture quickly at the commencement of their studies. Noteworthy comments include one student who felt that faculty in the host country favored students they liked and that grading standards were not in place to ensure equity. Another student remarked that the thing they missed most from their home country was the "freedom to break rules".

Table 8. What do you miss the most from your home country?

Category	Count	%	Remark
What do you miss the most from your home country?	29	32.2	Food as a single response
	12	12.2	Social interactions and communication
	7	7.1	Food
	5	5.1	The culture
	3	3.1	Non-verbal communication
	3	3.1	Not much similarity
	3	3.1	Racism

Noteworthy comments:

Uniform standard. While I like the flexibility in host country, it leaves open a lot of room for discrimination in host country. I have seen professors award As to students they like. Whereas in the home country, a lot of exams are graded in standardized ways to avoid discrimination. Since class grades are mostly exam focused, it leaves less wiggle room for professors to reward students they like better with better grades.

Freedom to break rules

Nothing, I hate my home country

Table 9. Students perception of what they will miss the most on returning to their home country

Category	Count	%	Remark
What do you miss the most from your host country when you return to your home country?	25	27.0	Life, lifestyle, culture responses
	7	7.6	Freedom, Democracy, Stability, or security
	5	5.4	My institution/the whole experience
	5	5.4	Opportunities - for improvement, advancement, education, and job.
	4	4.3	Weather/climate
	6	6.5	Mentioned their professors specifically

Noteworthy comments:

I liked the kind of culture my host country has, they are open to all culture, progressive and tolerant. They enjoy embracing variety of other cultures, food, traditions. I believe when I move to a metro and join a company I would come in touch with technologies and areas where I am interested to work. I think I am going to miss those areas when I return to my country. Also, there is huge difference in life style and amount of money that I earn here or will earn in future

The people themselves. I think the strong friendships I have built with my professors and peers are something of great value to me. I will miss seeing those faces later on in life. I will also miss [the institution] because it truly provides so many opportunities for students, whether it be free tuition, paid internships, advise on grad school, and so on. .... So, I will just miss the whole experience that I have had ... in its entirety.

None.

Finally, Table 9 shows what students will miss about the host country on returning to their home country. 27.0% of the respondents indicated that they would miss the lifestyle and culture. This suggests that the experience is a positive one for many students, but it does take some considerable time to adjust to, and accept, the culture of the host country.

7. Observations

Many of the identified problems are of the host institution's making. The comment made by one student regarding rote learning in a Master's program could be easily dismissed as one outlying opinion, but it may also signal an issue as more institutions move toward exams based on multiple choice questions to address the stress placed on faculty with large classes, high teaching loads, and the demands of US administrators to provide grades within 24 hours because of scholarship decisions and reporting functions require that information immediately.

Students coming from cultures where plagiarism is generally more accepted face significant challenges adjusting. Furthermore, an entire industry has evolved around helping students cheat or otherwise gain an unfair advantage over others [76, 98]. The temptation to use such devices and services is strong when other external factors such as financial pressures, or the need to perform in order to please family is considered. There are services to buy essays, and code; often these essays and program code are written to order making it difficult or impossible to detect the academic dishonesty that is occurring.

All faculty in a department need to enforce the same policies with respect to academic integrity, grading schemes. course workload, and expectations. Students often prefer to take courses with an "easy" instructor and there is a tendency to exploit the characteristics that make a particular instructor "easy". Faculty also need to be mindful of the message they send to the students and avoid questionable behavior that brings their own academic integrity into question. If there are standards that students are expected to adhere to, then all students need to be held to that standard, in all classes, and cases of student academic dishonesty should not be overlooked or handled outside of the advertised process.

There is a need to educate the domestic population about countries of the foreign students. Minimally, domestic students should know where these countries are and a little about what is happening in that region of the world. Institutions should cover local culture and help ease the transition from the culture of the home country to the host country by at least recognizing that the international students do not have a homogeneous background.

Conclusion

Practices and observations from the focus institutions, supported by survey results, and from previous bodies of work, highlight the challenges faced by international students and the challenge host institutions must address in order to successfully integrate them into the academic community. The examples show that the challenges are not unique to one host country, or one source country, but rather are a shared challenge faced by computing programs with significant international populations. International students enrich the campus, provide diversity in culture, thought, experience and perspective, and are often a revenue stream upon which some institutions are reliant. The ultimate challenge is maintaining and celebrating the diversity, while better integrating the students culturally and academically in order to reduce challenges and make the cultural and education experience more valuable to the international student, and to the domestic students that interact with them.

Student support is necessary prior to the start of the student's international experience. However, it is delivered at a time when retention and absorption of knowledge is impacted due to factors such as jet lag and being overwhelmed due to culture shock. On-going support is necessary. The fact that a topic is addressed during orientation does not mean that the student retains that information or even remembers that it was covered. The survey results support this.

International students are not a homogeneous group and should not be treated as such. For example, some may come from a privileged education background and others from more humble institutions, some may have language challenges, and others may experience a seismic shift in the educational experience they are asked to assimilate into. Orientation programs typically do not distinguish one international group from another. The typical orientation is to tell the students about the host country's culture and academic expectations without helping them make that transition quickly and seamlessly. Furthermore, the survey illustrated that attitudes to academic integrity appear to be independent of the source country.

Orientation addresses a number of matters that faculty regard as critical for the student's success. Issues covered include assimilation into the institution and academic integrity. However, in addition to having difficulty absorbing information at the time of orientation, there is an implicit assumption by the institution that the students are capable of suddenly suspending their home country's value system and their many years of previous experience in order to adopt the host country's values and to comply with the academic policies and processes of the host institution from that point forward. Expecting students to modify learned behavior and regionally accepted social and ethical behavior in order to instantaneously adopt the value system of the host institution and community is unrealistic, yet this is precisely what our expectation is when the orientation sessions are delivered immediately prior to the start of the student's first semester, and there is little or no follow-up afterwards.

Both faculty and students suffer from unconscious bias. Additional education is needed for the incoming international student to address their concerns regarding cultural and academic integration, but equally training for faculty on the challenges faced by international students, what they can expect in class, and how they can appropriately deal with the challenges as they arise is needed.

It is in the interest of students, faculty, and administrators to recognize the importance of academic integrity and to ensure that academic standards remain strong. Only by maintaining high standards of academic honesty can institutions protect the value of the educational process and the credibility of the institution and its graduates in the larger community.

Anecdotally, faculty who are well-traveled and empathetic to the student's challenges, but do not treat the international and domestic students differently in terms of deadlines, standards, expectations, and grading rubrics are helpful in bridging the gap faced by the student as they try to integrate into the host countries academic community and culture. Furthermore, differential treatment of the international and domestic students would create a double standard and violate academic integrity on behalf of the faculty. Such behavior would not be tolerated by the host institution. Consequently, fairly and appropriately addressing the cultural and integration challenges faced by a student in the classroom is difficult.

Future Work

This work was intended to be exploratory in nature. The results suggest that there is merit in a deeper investigation that addresses some of the limitations of this study.

This exploratory work does not rule out a connection between cultural and integration challenges, and observed behavior such as plagiarism which may be a indicator of those difficulties. Further work is needed to conclusively establish the connection and how it interferes with the students' academic success and potentially contributes to the pressure to engage in practices not deemed acceptable by the host institution. The work does suggest that more work needs to be done during orientation sessions to address changes in the educational system and expectations.

International students are not isolated on campus. They interact with domestic students, so a better understanding of the perceptions held by domestic students toward international students may provide helpful insights as the groups interact socially as well as academically.

The perception and experiences of international faculty (migrated after receiving qualifications, migrated after receiving qualifications in host country, and migrated before high school) of the challenges that international students face and the type of assistance the faculty provide, is also worth considering. Comparing and contrasting this to the perceptions and experiences of domestic faculty is also worth examining.

While this chapter has identified significant commonality in orientation procedures across the focus institutions, a more detailed study of effectiveness and impact is warranted. Eastern Institute of Technology is currently modifying its orientation procedure and placing some of the content into a required class that all international students must complete during the first four to six weeks of their first semester. a mechanism to try to ensure that students understand and retain information. Re-orientation week will occur at the start of every teaching period and engage students at all levels (freshmen to seniors). A review of these initiatives may show new directions for the orientation of international students.

Some institutions have students complete a year of language study to improve their proficiency in the host language prior to entering the degree studies. A comparison of the success of this cohort compared to those that enter the degree program immediately may provide insights into the value of a year of cultural immersion prior to focusing on their academic program.

A survey is also planned for students engaged in off-shore programs. These students remain in their local environment and the host institution delivers the program in the source country. From the delivering institution's perspective, the students are pursuing a degree from the host country and must adhere to the same rules as students who travel to the host country. This requires students to live in a community when attitudes toward academic integrity may differ from the expectations of the host institution. Such students typically lack peer support to help them adjust to the host institution's cultural norms and attitude toward academic integrity.

Only data related to computer science students was gathered in the survey conducted, and hence there is no basis to make the assertion that it applies to other disciplines - although we suspect it is. Much of the plagiarism that is detected and handled deals with written work and less so with programming. That is not to suggest that plagiarism does not takes place in coding assignments [100], just that there are less helpful tools to detect it. Further work is needed to conclusively tie cultural attitude to plagiarism, but this exploratory investigation does not rule it out.

References

[1] A. Kumi-Yeboah and W. James. Transformative learning experiences of international graduate students from Asian countries. *Journal of Transformative Education*, 12(1):25–53, 2014.

[2] J. J. C. H. Ryan. Plagiarism, graduate education, and information security. *IEEE Security and Privacy*, 5(5):62–65, September 2007.

[3] H. Marsden, M. Carroll, and J. T. Neill. Who cheats at university? A self-report study of dishonest academic behaviours in a sample of Australian university students. *Journal of Psychology*, 57:1–10, 2005.

[4] D. L. McCabe. Cheating among college and university students: A North American perspective. *International Journal for Educational Integrity*, 1(1), 2005.

[5] P. Ashworth, P. Bannister, P. Thorne, and students on the Qualitative Research Methods Course Unit. Guilty in whose eyes? University students' perceptions of cheating and plagiarism in academic work and assessment. *Studies in Higher Education*, 22(2):187–203, 1997. http://dx.doi.org/10.1080/03075079712331381034.

[6] F. Awuah. Plagiarism is a crime: towards academic integrity in higher educational institutions in Ghana. *British Journal of Education*, 4(12):1–12, 2016.

[7] Y. Zhou, D. Jindal-Snape, K. Topping, and J. Todman. Theoretical models of culture shock and adaptation in international students in higher education. *Studies in Higher Education*, 33(1):63–75, 2008.

[8] J. Carter. Collaboration or plagiarism: What happens when students work together. In B. Manaris, editor, *4th Annual SIGCSE/SIGCUE Conference on Innovation and Technology in Computer Science Education (ITICSE 99)*, pages 52–55. Association of Computing Machinery, Krakow, Poland, 1999.

[9] S. Weller. Understanding unintentional plagiarism and international students' approaches to academic reading: a participatory approach to researching the international student experience. Project report, The Higher Education Academy, UK, 2013.

[10] G. S. K. Adika. Credibility and accountability in academic discourse: increasing the awareness of ghanaian graduate students. *Practice and Theory in Systems of Education*, 10(3):227–244, 2015.

[11] S. G. K. Adika. Ghanaian graduate students' knowledge of referencing in academic writing and implications for plagiarism. *Frontiers of Language and Teaching*, 5:75–80, 2014.

[12] G. Hofstede. National culture and corporate cultures. In L. A. Samovar and R. E. Porter, editors, *Communication between cultures*. Belmont, CA, Wadsworth, 1984.

[13] Z. Abukari. *Awareness and incidence of plagiarism among students of higher education: a case study of Narh-Bita College*. PhD thesis, University of Ghana, Department of Information Studies, 2016.

[14] The Higher Education Academy. Plagiarism and collusion. The Higher Education Academy, 2005. https://www.heacademy.ac.uk/knowledge-hub/quick-guide-plagiarism-and-collusion.

[15] JISC Internet Plagiarism Advisory Service. Reducing plagiarism through assessment design. Technical report, York St John University, 2003. https://www.yorksj.ac.uk/media/content-assets/academic-development/documents/Assessment-Designs.pdf.

[16] J. Sheard and M. Dick. Directions and dimensions in managing cheating and plagiarism in it students. In *Proceedings of the Fourteenth Australasian Computing Education Conference (ACE)*, volume 123, pages 177–186, Melbourne, Australia, 2012.

[17] J. Sheard and M. Dick. Influences of cheating practices on graduate students in it courses: what are the factors? In *Annual Conference on Innovation and Technology in Computer Science Education*. ACM, 2003.

[18] J. Sheard and M. Dick. Computing student practices of cheating and plagiarism: a decade of change. In *ITiCSE'11 Proceedings of the 16th annual joint conference of Innovation and Technology in Computer Science Education*, pages 233–237, Darmstadt, Germany, July 2011.

[19] M. Dick, J. Sheard, C. Bareiss, J. Carter, D. Joyce, T. Harding, and C. Laxer. Addressing student cheating: definitions and solutions. *ACM SIGCSE Bulletin*, 35(2):172–184, 2003.

[20] J. Sheard, Simon, Butler M., Falkner K., and M. Morgan. Strategies for maintaining academic integrity in first-year computing courses. In *22nd Annual Conference on Innovation and Technology in Computer Science Education (ITiCSE)*, pages 244–249, Bologna, Italy, July 2017. ACM.

[21] J. Bamford and K. Sergiou. International students and plagiarism: an analysis of the reasons for plagiarism among international foundation stu-

dents. *Investigations in University Teaching and Learning*, 4(12):17–22, 2005.

[22] The Higher Education Academy. *Addressing plagiarism: teaching international students project*. The Higher Education Academy, UK, 2014. https://www.heacademy.ac.uk/system/files/resources/addressing_plagiarism.pdf.

[23] J. Pierce and C. Zilles. Investigating student plagiarism patterns and correlations to grades. In *ACM SIGCSE'17*, pages 471–476, Seattle, WA, March 2017.

[24] E. Denisova-Schmidt. The global challenge of academic integrity. *eJournal of International Higher Education Fall*, 87:4–6, September 2016. https://ejournals.bc.edu/ojs/index.php/ihe/article/view/9514/8479.

[25] E. Denisova-Schmidt. Facing up to international students who cheat. *University World News*, 23, September 2016. http://www.universityworldnews.com/article.php?story=201609211256-27336.

[26] E. Denisova-Schmidt. *The Challenges of Academic Integrity in Higher Education: Current Trends and Prospects*, volume 5. The Boston College Center for International Higher Education (CIHE), Chestnut Hill, MA, June 2017. https://www.alexandria.unisg.ch/251258/.

[27] W. Tierney and N. Sabharwal. Analyzing corruption in Indian higher education. *University World News*, September 2016. http://www.universityworldnews.com/article.php?story=201609211256-27336.

[28] W. G. Tierney and N. S. Sabharwal. Academic corruption: Culture and trust in Indian higher education. *International Journal of Educational Development*, 55(C):30–40, 2017. https://EconPapers.repec.org/RePEc:eee:injoed:v:55:y:2017:i:c:p:30-40.

[29] C. O. Oppong. Education and intercultural relations: a case study of ghanaian and nigerian students in finland. *Technical report*, University of Eastern Finland, 2016.

[30] A. Berglund and N. Thota. A glimpse into the cultural situatedness of computer science: Some insights from a pilot study. In *2014 International Conference on Teaching and Learning in Computing and Engineering*, pages 92–99, April 2014. http://ieeexplore.ieee.org/document/6821835/.

[31] J. Russell, D. Rosenthal, and G. Thomson. The international student experience: Three styles of adaptation. *Higher Education*, 60(2):235–249, 2010.

[32] S. Bochner, B. M. McLeod, and A. Lin. Friendship patterns of overseas students: A functional model. *International Journal of Psychology*, 12(4):277–294, 1977.

[33] B. Rienties, S. Beausaert, T. Grohnert, S. Niemantsverdriet, and P. Kommers. Understanding academic performance of international students: the role of ethnicity, academic and social integration. *Higher Education*, 63(6):685–700, 2012.

[34] A. T. Church. Sojourner adjustment. *Psychological Bulletin*, 91(3):540–572, 1982. http://www.apa.org/pubs/journals/bul/.

[35] C. Ward, S. Bochner, and A. Furnham. *The psychology of culture shock*. Routledge, East Sussex, England, second edition, 2001.

[36] R. Nisbett. *The Geography of Thought: How Asians and Westerners Think Differently*. Simon and Schuster, 2004.

[37] J. Campbell and M. Li. Asian students' voices: an empirical study of Asian students' learning experiences at a New Zealand university. *Journal of Studies in International Education*, 12(4):375–396, 2008.

[38] Institute of International Education. Attitudes and perceptions of prospective international students from Vietnam. *An IIE briefing paper, Institute of International Education*, 2010. https://www.iie.org/Research-and-Insights/Publications/Briefing-Paper-2010-Vietnam.

[39] S. Alaoutinen and K. Smolander. Are computer science students different learners. In *Koli Calling '10, Proceedings of the 10th Koli Calling*

Conference on Computing Education Research, pages 100–105, October 2010.

[40] R. Rosenthal and L. Jacobsen. *Pygmalian in the Classroom.* Holt, Rinehart & Winston, New York, 1968.

[41] T. Inamori and F. Analoui. Beyond pygmalion effect: the role of managerial perception. *Journal of Management Development*, 29(4):306–321, 2010.

[42] C. Anderson, R. Arshad, and J. Hancock. *Internationalising the higher education framework.* The Higher Education Academy, UK, 2016.

[43] J. Lu, J. Yao, K. L. Chin, J. Xiao, and J. Xu. *Strategies and approaches to teaching and learning cross cultures.* Australian Learning and Teaching Council, Sydney, Australia, 2010.

[44] B. Crump. New arrival students: mitigating factors on the culture of the computing learning environment. In R. Lister and A. Young, editors, *ACE 2004, 6th Australian Computing Education Conference*, volume 30 of *Conferences in Research and Practice in Information Technology*, pages 49–56, Dunedin, New Zealand, January 2004.

[45] B. Crump. The new arrival minority: perceptions of their first-year tertiary programming environment. *Journal of Women and Minorities in Science and Engineering*, 10(1):21–35, 2004.

[46] K. Egea, J. Lu., J. Xiao, and T. Clear. Internationalisation and cross cultural issues in computing education. In T. Clear and J. Hamer, editors, *ACE 2010, 12th Australasian Computing Education Conference*, volume 103 of *Conferences in Research and Practice in Information Technology*, pages 25–32, Brisbane, Australia, January 2010.

[47] L. Gardenswartz and A. Rowe. *The managing diversity survival guide.* Irwin Professional Publishing, Burr Ridge, IL, 1994.

[48] Institute of International Education. Advising international students in an age of anxiety. *An IIE white paper, Institute of International Education, March 2017.* https://www.iie.org/Research-and-Insights/Publications/Advising-Students-in-an-Age-of-Anxiety.

[49] C. Y. Oh and B. S. Butler. Newcomers from the other side of the globe: international students' local information seeking during adjustment. In *ASIST 2016, Annual Meeting of the Association for Information Science and Technology*, Copenhagen, Denmark, October 2016.

[50] C. Ward and A. Masgoret. The experiences of international students in New Zealand: Report on the results of the national survey. *Technical report, Prepared for the Ministry of Education, June 2004*. http://www.educationcounts.govt.nz/publications/international/14700.

[51] C. Ward and A. Masgoret. Attitudes towards immigrants, immigration, and multiculturalism in New Zealand: A social psychological analysis. *International Migration Review (IMR)*, 42(1):227–248, 2007.

[52] C. Ward, Y. Okura, A. Kennedy, and T. Kojima. The u-curve on trial: A longitudinal study of the psychological and sociocultural adjustment during cross-cultural transition. *International Journal of Intercultural Relations*, 22(3):277–291, 1998.

[53] J. Carter, D. Bouvier, R. Cardell-Oliver, M. Hamilton, S. Kurkovsky, S. Markham, O. W. McClung, R. McDermott, R. Riedesel, J. Shi, and S. White. Motivating all our students? In *Proceedings of the 16th Annual Conference Reports on Innovation and Technology in Computer Science Education - Working Group Reports, ITiCSE-WGR '11*, pages 1–18, New York, NY, USA, 2011. ACM.

[54] M. Lynch. *Examining the impact of culture on academic performance.* Huffington Post, October 2011. https://www.huffingtonpost.com/matthew-lynch-edd/education-culture_b_1034197.html.

[55] N. Hayes and L. Introna. Alienation and plagiarism: Coping with otherness in our assessment practice. *Technical report, Lancaster University, UK, 2004*.

[56] L. Introna, N. Hayes, L. Blair, and E. Wood. Cultural attitudes towards plagiarism: Developing a better understanding of the needs of students from diverse cultural backgrounds relating to plagiarism. *Technical report, Lancaster University, UK, 2003*.

[57] R. Choudaha. Campus readiness for supporting international student success. *Journal of International Students*, 6(4), 2016.

[58] C. Newstead, R. Gann, S. Kirk, and C. Rounsaville. *Disciplinary perspectives on internationalising the curriculum*. The Higher Education Academy, UK, 2016.

[59] N. Thota and A. Berglund. At the crossroad of computer science and intercultural interactions: A framework for analysis and interpretation. In *EARLI SIG 9 Conference on Phenomenography and Variation Theory*, Jönköping University, Sweden, August 2012.

[60] N. Thota and A. Berglund. Learning computer science: Dimensions of variation within what Chinese students learn. *ACM Transactions on Computing Education*, 16(3):1–27, 2016.

[61] J. G. Graham. English language proficiency and the prediction of academic success. *TESOL quarterly*, 21(3):505–521, 1987.

[62] P. Johnson. English language proficiency and academic performance of undergraduate international students. *TESOL quarterly*, 22(1):164–168, 1988.

[63] R. Baron. *The first year international student perception and experience of employability: a case of tourism and hospitality students*. Master's thesis, Deakin University School of Education, Melbourne, Australia, 2016.

[64] M. J. Bennett. A developmental approach to training for intercultural sensitivity. *International Journal of Intercultural Relations*, 10:179–186, 1986.

[65] J. Carroll. Institutional issues in deterring, detecting and dealing with student plagiarism. *JISC briefing paper*, 2004.

[66] E. Gómez Parra. "Cultural distance" among speakers of the same language. *Sens Public*, October 2009. http://www.sens-public.org/article653.html?lang=fr.

[67] S. Abufarehm. KM and global software engineering (GSE). In S. Saeed and I. Alsmadi, editors, *Knowledge-based Processes in Software Development*, chapter 2, pages 12–34. IGI Global, 2013.

[68] J. D. Herbsleb, D. Paulish, and M. Bass. Global software development at siemens: experience from nine projects. In *Proceedings of the 27th International Conference on Software Engineering*, pages 524–533, MO, USA, 2005. St. Louis.

[69] S. B. Sanna, E. Ablordeppey, N. J. Mensah, and T. K. Karikari. Academic dishonesty in higher education: students? Perceptions and involvement in an African institution. *BioMed Central: BMC Research Notes*, 9(1):234, 2016.

[70] BBC News. 'Plagiarist' to sue university, May 2004. http://news.bbc.co.uk/2/hi/uk_news/education/3753065.stm.

[71] J. Lu, K. L. Chin, J. Yao, J. Xu, and J. Xiao. Cross-cultural education: learning methodology and behavior analysis for Asian students in IT field of Australian universities. In T. Clear and J. Hamer, editors, *ACE 2010, 12th Australasian Computing Education Conference*, volume 103, pages 117–126, Brisbane, Australia, January 2010.

[72] A. Mostrous and B. Kenber. Universities face student cheating crisis. *The Times Newspaper*, January 2016. https://www.thetimes.co.uk/article/universities-face-student-cheating-crisis-9jt6ncd9vz7.

[73] R. Iyengar. Dozens scale school walls in india to help students cheat in exams. *Time magazine*, March 2015. http://time.com/3752128/india-bihar-exam-cheating-climbing-walls/.

[74] *The Telegraph*. Indian army tackles cheating by making 1,000 candidates take exam in underwear in field, March 2016. http://www.telegraph.co.uk/news/worldnews/asia/india/12180174/Indian-army-tackles-cheating-by-making-1000-candidates-take-exam-in-underwear-in-field.html.

[75] K. J. Shashidhar. Gujarat bans mobile internet to prevent cheating in an exam. *Medianama*, 2006. http://www.medianama.com/2016/02/223-gujarat-bans-mobile-internet-to-prevent-cheating-in-an-exam/.

[76] K. H. Qing, A. Harney, S. Stecklow, and J. Pomfret. How an industry helps Chinese students cheat their way into and through U.S. colleges. *Reuters*, May 2016. http://www.reuters.com/investigates/special-report/college-cheating-iowa/.

[77] L. Hitchcock, Q. Vu, and D. Tran. Intercultural competence in practice: Reflections on establishing cross-cultural collaborative education programmes. *ACM Inroads*, 1(3):85–93, 2010.

[78] G. Hofstede and G. J. Hofstede. *Cultures and organization: Software of the mind*. McGraw Hill, New York, NY, 2005.

[79] J. W. Berry. Acculturation. living successfully in two cultures. *International Journal of Intercultural Relations*, 29:697–712, 2005.

[80] G. Alred. Becoming a 'better stranger': A therapeutic perspective on intercultural education and/as education. In G. Alfred, M. Byram, and M. Fleming, editors, *Intercultural experience and education. Languages for intercultural communication and education*, chapter 2, pages 14–30. Multilingual Matters Ltd, Clevedon, England, 2003.

[81] D. Bender-Szymanski. Learning through cultural conflict? a longitudinal analysis of german teachers' strategies for coping with cultural diversity in schools. *European Journal of Teacher Education*, 23(3):229–250, 2000.

[82] R. Fischer and A. Mansell. Commitment across cultures: A meta-analytical approach. *Journal of International Business Studies*, 40, 2009.

[83] G. H. Hofstede. *Culture's consequences: International differences in work-related values*. Sage Publications, Beverly Hills, CA, 1980.

[84] G. H. Hofstede. *Culture's Consequences: Comparing Values, Behaviors, Institutions, and Organizations across Nations*. Sage, Thousand Oaks, CA, 2nd and enlarged edition, 2001.

[85] D. Oyserman and A. K. Uskul. Individualism and collectivism: Societal-level processes with implications for individual-level and societal-level outcomes. In F. van de Vijver, D. A. van Hemert, and Y. H. Poortinga, editors, *Multilevel analysis of individuals and cultures*, chapter 6. *Psychology Press*, Lawrence Erlbaum Associates, New York, NY, 2015.

[86] L. Reid. The importance of Hofstede's dimensions of culture. *Penn State Leadership in Global Context Cultural Leadership Blog*, 2015. http://sites.psu.edu/global/2015/04/25/the-importance-of-hofstedes-dimensions-of-culture/.

[87] F. Trompenaars and C. Hampton-Turner. *Riding the waves of culture: Understanding diversity in global business (2nd ed.)*. McGraw-Hill, New York, NY, 1998.

[88] R. D. Lewis. *When cultures collide: Leading across cultures*. Nicholas Brealey International, Boston, MA, third edition, 2006.

[89] M. Bennett. Towards ethnorelativism: A developmental model of intercultural sensitivity. In R. M. Paige, editor, *Education for the intercultural experience*. Intercultural Press, Inc., Boston, MA, 1993.

[90] M. Blasco. On reflection: Is reflexivity necessarily beneficial in intercultural education? *Intercultural Education*, 23(6):475–489, 2012.

[91] A. Pearson-Evans. Recording the journey: Diaries of Irish students in japan. In M. Byram and A Feng, editors, *Living and studying abroad: Research and practice. Languages for intercultural communication and education*. Multilingual Matters Ltd, Clevedon, England, 2006.

[92] S. Bochner, N. Hutnick, and A. Furnham. The friendship patterns of overseas and host students in oxford student residence. *The Journal of Social Psychology*, 125(6):689–694, 1985.

[93] G. Weaver. Understanding and coping with cross-cultural adjustment stress. In R. M. Paige, editor, *Education for the intercultural experience*. Maine Intercultural Press, Inc., Yarmouth, ME, 1993.

[94] J. Shaules. *'Deep Culture': The hidden challenges of global living. Languages for intercultural communication and education.* Multilingual Matters Ltd, Clevedon, England, 2007.

[95] Worcester State University. *Citations.* Worcester State University, Worcester, MA, 2017. http://libguides.worcester.edu/citations.

[96] Berea College. *Academic honesty statement.* Berea College, 2018. http://catalog.berea.edu/en/Current/Shared-Content/Academic-Honesty-Dishonesty.

[97] Northwest Missouri State University. *Academic integrity policy.* School of Computer Science and Information Systems, 2018. http://www.nwmissouri.edu/csis/pdf/AcademicIntegrityCSI.pdf.

[98] R. Chugh. Students are using 'smart' spy technology to cheat in exams. *Science Alert*, 2016. http://www.sciencealert.com/students-are-using-smart-spy-technology-to-cheat-in-exams.

[99] M. K. Appiah. The evil that men do in academics: Understanding plagiarism and its extenuating circumstances. *British Journal of Education*, 4(6):56–67, 2016. http://www.eajournals.org/wp-content/uploads/The-Evil-that-Men-Do-in-Academics.pdf.

[100] G. Cosma, M. Joy, J. Sinclair, M. Andreou, D. Zhang, B. Cook, and R. Boyatt. Perceptual comparison of source-code plagiarism within students from uk, china, and south cyprus higher education institutions. *Transactions on Computing Education*, 17(2):16 pages, May 2017. Article B.

INDEX

A

academic adjustment, viii, 48, 49, 51, 53, 55, 58, 59, 62, 64, 65, 68, 135
academic stresses, vii, ix, 77, 78, 79, 80, 82, 86, 89, 90, 91, 92
acculturation, 11, 15, 18, 20, 29, 30, 50, 69, 75
acculturative stress, 4, 11, 12, 15, 43, 54, 75, 79, 89, 90
activity, 60, 152
adjustment, vii, viii, 2, 4, 7, 10, 13, 14, 16, 19, 20, 22, 29, 30, 31, 38, 42, 43, 48, 49, 50, 51, 52, 53, 54, 55, 56, 57, 58, 59, 60, 61, 62, 63, 64, 65, 67, 68, 69, 70, 72, 73, 74, 75, 80, 81, 82, 90, 135, 141, 142, 175, 177, 181
analysis, 7, 16, 19, 35, 43, 54, 57, 63, 108, 130, 173, 177, 178, 179, 180, 181
Asian international students, viii, 1, 2, 3, 12, 34, 37, 39, 72

B

best friend relationship, 85, 86, 88

bicultural identity, 7, 19, 21, 30
bicultural model, 2
bicultural self, 7

C

case study, 17, 57, 58, 59, 75, 136, 173, 174
China, 3, 5, 6, 8, 10, 12, 30, 31, 34, 40, 43, 78, 79, 93, 96, 110, 130, 156
Chinese, v, ix, 3, 5, 6, 7, 13, 16, 18, 19, 20, 21, 29, 30, 31, 34, 36, 38, 39, 40, 41, 42, 43, 44, 45, 60, 68, 71, 72, 73, 77, 78, 79, 80, 82, 85, 87, 89, 90, 91, 92, 93, 94, 95, 96, 97, 132, 135, 156, 178, 180
Chinese international students, ix, 3, 30, 42, 68, 71, 73, 78, 79, 80, 87, 89, 91, 92
classroom interaction, 59, 62
collectivistic, 7, 20, 23, 24, 26, 27, 28, 29, 30
community, 15, 20, 52, 53, 60, 63, 65, 69, 72, 80, 81, 133, 138, 141, 143, 145, 148, 153, 168, 169, 171
competency, 15, 42, 84, 86, 135
counseling, 3, 33, 37, 39, 40, 74, 75, 91
cross-cultural, 3, 17, 19, 21, 23, 24, 26, 32, 35, 43, 59, 60, 68, 71

cross-national cultural competency, 15
cultural sensitivity, 4, 32, 181
culture shock, x, 4, 11, 13, 35, 53, 60, 69, 73, 126, 132, 143, 144, 145, 168, 172, 175

D

depression, 4, 11, 15, 36, 41, 42, 54, 55, 61
discrimination, 3, 15, 20, 52, 60, 62, 63, 132, 135, 166

E

English names, 16, 18
English proficiency, ix, 15, 77, 80, 89, 91, 92, 135
ethnicity, 7, 18, 29, 38, 68, 70, 175
expectations, vii, ix, x, 19, 21, 24, 69, 83, 89, 90, 91, 99, 101, 103, 108, 113, 114, 117, 118, 126, 127, 129, 130, 132, 134, 140, 142, 149, 151, 152, 158, 159, 160, 163, 167, 168, 169, 170, 171
experiences and expectations, 100, 134
exploratory sequential mixed methods design (ESMMD), 56, 57

F

face, 4, 13, 19, 23, 25, 28, 38, 39, 45, 80, 126, 131, 133, 134, 136, 137, 138, 142, 144, 145, 151, 152, 154, 156, 157, 167, 170, 179
follow-up, 100, 108, 114, 117, 118
forbearance, 25, 30, 39
friend, 33, 85, 86, 88, 90, 161
functional adjustment, 11, 14

G

globalization, 7, 20, 48, 101, 104, 113, 115, 120
group harmony, 19, 23, 24, 27, 30

H

happiness, 52, 61, 63
homesickness, 12, 15, 54, 61, 63, 80, 137
human capital, 26, 27, 28, 100, 103

I

identity, 6, 7, 8, 13, 15, 18, 19, 21, 29, 30, 31, 34, 36, 37, 38, 41, 55, 72, 142, 156
indigenous psychology, viii, 2, 4, 22, 25, 28, 30
individualism, 7, 17, 21, 40
International Students Adjustment Scale (ISAS), 57, 58, 61

L

language anxiety, 4, 11, 13, 38, 41
language proficiency, 9, 17, 74, 78, 80, 89, 110, 178
learning, 2, 13, 16, 19, 39, 42, 50, 51, 55, 59, 62, 63, 65, 71, 72, 79, 101, 108, 113, 114, 120, 132, 136, 139, 142, 143, 150, 151, 158, 160, 161, 162, 163, 167, 171, 175, 176, 179
learning styles, 16, 136
locus of control, 22, 25, 26, 30, 33, 35, 41
loneliness, ix, 13, 54, 56, 61, 63, 78, 80, 81, 84, 86, 87, 89, 91, 137

Index

M

Malaysian International University Students' (MIUSs'), 56, 57, 58, 59, 61, 64, 65
mental health, 11, 12, 13, 14, 16, 25, 27, 29, 31, 32, 33, 34, 39, 54, 65, 74
mental illness, 11, 13, 14, 16, 31
Mien-tzu, 28

N

national identity, 7
nationality, 7, 18, 20, 29, 31, 52, 130, 136

O

outbound exchange students, vii, ix, 99, 107, 113, 114
outbound students, 100, 101, 106, 107, 108, 115, 116, 117, 122
outcomes of international, 101, 103

P

parental involvement, 84, 86, 87, 89, 91
parental support, 84, 86, 87, 90
Pearson product-moment correlation, 63
peer group relationship, 85, 86, 87, 88
perceived English fluency, 11, 36
perceptions of workload and examinations, 83, 85, 87
pressure to perform, 86, 87
priority difference, 22, 23
psychological adjustment, vii, viii, 31, 40, 48, 50, 53, 54, 55, 56, 58, 61, 62, 63, 64, 65, 69, 70, 71, 81, 90

Q

qualitative, 4, 11, 16, 17, 18, 19, 56, 58, 71, 72
quantitative, 10, 16, 56, 75

R

race, 7, 29
Ren-qing, 27
resilience, 20, 22, 26, 31, 54

S

satisfaction with life, 14, 15, 116, 117
self-perceptions, 83, 85, 88
social adjustment, 48, 65
social capital, 26, 27, 28, 34, 42
social support, 3, 36, 53, 55, 56, 64, 70, 74, 75, 78, 79, 81, 89, 90, 92, 116, 122
stress, 4, 11, 12, 34, 42, 53, 54, 55, 61, 63, 64, 70, 80, 81, 82, 83, 87, 89, 90, 128, 132, 142, 159, 167, 181
student mobility, 66, 100, 101, 102, 103, 104, 105, 106, 114, 117, 118, 121
students who are non-mobile, 118
support systems, 22, 27, 30, 33, 35, 53
Sweden, v, vii, ix, 99, 100, 105, 106, 107, 108, 109, 115, 117, 119, 121, 122, 123, 124, 135, 178

T

Taiwan, 3, 5, 6, 7, 8, 9, 10, 12, 16, 18, 21, 22, 25, 29, 30, 34, 35, 36, 37, 39, 40, 43, 44, 45
Taiwanese, v, vii, viii, 1, 2, 3, 4, 5, 6, 7, 8, 9, 10, 11, 12, 13, 14, 15, 16, 17, 18, 19, 20, 21, 22, 23, 24, 25, 26, 27, 28, 29, 30,

31, 32, 33, 34, 35, 36, 37, 38, 39, 40, 41, 42, 43, 45, 72
Taiwanese International Bicultural Model (TIBM), v, viii, 1, 2, 4, 20, 22, 29, 30, 31, 32, 34
Taiwanese international students, vii, viii, 2, 3, 4, 7, 8, 9, 10, 11, 12, 13, 14, 15, 16, 18, 19, 22, 23, 24, 25, 27, 28, 29, 30, 31, 32, 33, 34, 36, 41, 42, 72
teaching, x, 9, 19, 39, 51, 55, 59, 60, 62, 65, 79, 114, 126, 132, 135, 137, 138, 139, 144, 153, 154, 162, 163, 164, 167, 170, 174, 176
time restraints, 83, 85, 88

U

undergraduate international students, 78, 178
university service and administration, 59
US institutions, 79, 82

Y

young Chinese, vii, ix, 77, 78, 79, 80, 82, 87, 88, 89, 90, 91, 92
young Chinese undergraduates, 79
young sojourners, 82, 88, 90, 91